ELEVEN AS ONE

ONE

Memoirs of a Grateful Jewish Mother

Yael Gollub

iUniverse, Inc.
Bloomington

Eleven as One
Memoirs of a Grateful Jewish Mother

Copyright © 2011 Yael Gollub

iUniverse books may be ordered through booksellers or by contacting:

iUniverse
1663 Liberty Drive
Bloomington, IN 47403
www.iuniverse.com
1-800-Authors (1-800-288-4677)

Because of the dynamic nature of the Internet, any Web addresses or links contained in this book may have changed since publication and may no longer be valid. The views expressed in this work are solely those of the author and do not necessarily reflect the views of the publisher, and the publisher hereby disclaims any responsibility for them.

ISBN: 978-1-4620-0728-8 (pbk)
ISBN: 978-1-4620-0729-5 (ehk)

Printed in the United States of America

iUniverse rev. date: 7/8/2011

I would like to dedicate this book to my sister-in-law
Ainat Emeth and a great teacher G. Donnell, for believing
in me and encouraging me to write this book.

Chapter 1

My life is like a runaway train most days. My neighbor says I remind her of the Tasmanian Devil and the coyote that chases the roadrunner—both cartoon characters. I don't know if that is a compliment, but I agree with her, for she never, *ever* sees me sit and relax, even for a minute.

I start my day at the gym usually, going to the 5:45 a.m. cycling class. One day, the instructor was making us go uphill, and after five minutes, she said, "Okay, if you have one child, come down … If you have two, come down … If you have three, come down … If you have four, come down …" Out of fifty people, I was the only one still cycling. She continued cautiously, "Five … six …" I could feel everyone's eyeballs on me. "Seven … eight …" Finally giving up, she questioned, "How many kids do you have?"

I could not answer right away because I was scared of the reaction, but the dead silence in the room was worse. Out of breath, I proudly answered, "I have eleven." A six-foot black man was smiling and shaking his head from side to side; the others said the number eleven repeatedly; and the teacher, about four feet tall, blond, and probably weighing one hundred and twenty pounds, got off her bike and bowed to me, saying, "You can sit anytime." (The oldest of my children is Shimon, thirty-six; then Devorah, thirty-five; Shoshana, thirty-four; Larry, thirty-two; Sophie, thirty; Pennina, thirty; Miriam, twenty-five; Rivka, twenty-

1

two; Alvin, twenty-one; Yaacove, nineteen; and finally, Hadassah, fourteen.I have four boys and seven girls.) Very rarely do I sit and just do nothing!

I can recall one typical day, waking up my crew and sending some of them off with a smile, making sure they had all their belongings so I wouldn't have to make a second trip to school. Within seconds, I was on high alert. Yaccove had a dentist appointment at eight forty-five that morning; Ruthy, my daughter-in-law, called me at seven thirty to ask if my grandsons (three and five years old) could tag along until two o'clock. I cordially said, "I'll pick them up after the dentist." Yaacove would have to walk home after his orthodontist check up.

By nine thirty, I went from one kid to three. I was expecting to do morning prayer and make breakfast for my husband and me, but he dropped a bomb as I opened the front door. "You're overdrawn at the bank by a thousand dollars. Here's a check to cover some of it."

I wanted to scream and run away. Without saying a word, I grabbed the check from David, and back out I went to the car, leaving my husband to babysit for a few minutes. I rushed to the bank around the corner from us.

William, a middle-aged man with a cheerful face, smiled and said, "It's only nine thirty in the morning and you're overdrawn by a thousand dollars."

I briefly thought about how I had just come back from Florida and spent some money on bagels, paper goods, and one meal, which my Shoshana and I shared, at a restaurant. However, that was barely $100. I sighed as he printed out a sheet and casually continued speaking. "You had Chase take out $750 ... and $1,506.24 a week later."

Before I could breathe, I yelled, "Impossible! They don't have this account. We are on debt reduction plan. It is part of a consumer law group that reduced our interest on our credit cards , and they only take from the other account ... and it's only the twenty-seventh of each month."

With nothing to do, I took the printout and zoomed home. I got my folder out and called Chase, only to hear them say, "Yes, we have the $750 payment showing but no $1,506.24."

I felt as if I were dead. I could not talk, and I just started to cry. Finally, I said, "That's my food money. I have one account for bills and one for household needs. You touched the household account, that's not the account you guys can take out of. I did not give you permission."

The woman on the other side was as cold as ice. "Lady, I'm trying to help you. If you keep yelling at me, I can't help you."

My voice got louder. "I'm not yelling—I'm crying."

"Hold on, please."

I was holding on, but based on past experience, it never works; I always get cut off after holding on for five to ten minutes. I could not help it, and again a gush of tears escaped from my eyes. My mind was racing faster than the cars in the Indy 500.

Finally, she came back on the phone. "Do you know a Mr. S. Lander?"

My heart stopped, and I forced myself to answer yes.

"Well, ma'am, he took the money out of your account and paid his Chase account."

As if she would have the answer, I yelled, "Why would he do that?"

"Ma'am, just call your bank and explain that you did not authorize that payment."

I called Shimon, my son, on the phone. I knew he would be teaching, but I took a chance. He did not answer. I called my daughter-in-law. She listened patiently, calmly, and sympathetically.

"I don't know why Shimon would do such a thing. He was paying bills; maybe he mistakenly put your account number instead of his … Do you want me to write you a check? I'll give you as much as you need, Emah." (She and others call me that; it means *mother* in Hebrew.) Her soft English accent calmed me down. I started to breathe normally.

"Okay, it's a mistake," I said. "I'll get the money back today before the banks close."

After grabbing whatever energy I had, I packed up the car with three kids, and off I went on the 405 freeway, heading toward the school to meet with the teachers of my youngest child, Hadassa. Hadassa had voiced her opinion earlier that morning about my coming to her school. "As soon as you hear I didn't do well in math or reading, you'll embarrass me in front of Denial and Shalom" (my grandkids). I promised I would not do that, and anyway, while I was with the teachers, someone had to take care of the two little ones I had tagging along. When we reached the front of the school grounds, the kids ran to the playground. I asked Hadassa to go watch them.

Feeling rather confident, I walked into a room decorated with pictures of trees, a huge calendar, and Hebrew letters (the kind I cannot read, in Rashi script). Then my daughter's picture grabbed my attention. It had a note about special wishes: *I wish my mom were rich and I want twelve children and Mashiach should come now.*

One of the teachers commented that Hadassa had turned around 180 degrees. I sank in my chair and sighed. If only they knew how hard it was for me to get her to learn her math and read Hebrew. The one thing she had started to enjoy was her Chumash (the first book of Genesis). She could pick out words that she had learned in class in her prayer book. The teacher went on to let me know that she was a very smart young lady, and that I should stop calling her "my little baby."

I dared to ask her English teacher how her reading level was. To my surprise, the tall blonde woman with her doctorate degree in reading showed me a huge smile with all her straight white teeth. "She's reading eighty-one words a minute; she needs to be at ninety. I'm not worried," she declared, patting me on the back for doing a great job with her. I got up to leave and gave each teacher a hug.

The Hebrew teacher, Rose Green, from London, England, whom I have known for thirty years, walked out with me, and I was a little suspicious as to why she was accompanying me out. As we turned the corner from the classroom, she whispered, "Check her hair, Yael. She's still itching." Talk about a balloon bursting.

My oldest daughter had volunteered to work in camp for a girl that is ultra Orthodox. She lived in New York. For three months before she was to fly to New York it was hard for me to see my sixteen-year-old cry and yell, "I'm going to have a lousy summer." I begged her to say that her mom did not want her to go. It turned out worse, she did not get paid for the job and she came home with a lot of company … tiny creatures called *lice*.

I tried to get rid of it for weeks, but it just did not go away. Talk about missing math, history, and Hebrew. My oldest daughter, Devorah, took her home one Saturday night and, no lie, stayed with her until three in the morning, taking out nits. I joined them on Sunday, but Devorah told Rivka sternly that under no circumstances would she even attempt to get rid of any more lice until she cut her long, curly blonde hair.

Off to the haircut we went. My daughter and I both worried that the woman would notice the plague … and then what? Thank G-d she didn't. My Rivka got a haircut as well as bangs, which she had not asked for. The tears never stopped, and of course, it was my fault for her bangs, missing school, and that I was unable to see the microscopic creatures. My kind and understanding husband could not take his little girl crying, not Rivka, who thinks only of others.

When Rivka was four, we were at my only nephew's third birthday party, which is the traditional time for a child to receive his first haircut. Yosef, one of my favorite cousins, was giving out kosher Mickey Mouse lollipops to all the little kids. No sooner had he passed out his last one than the birthday boy, David (named after my father), reached out his hand confidently. There was no reciprocation from my cousin. Not knowing what to do, he came to me and explained what had just transpired. Without blinking an eye I said, "Let's go ask Rivka for hers." My little American Jewish doll took her last lick, and we cannot believe to this day what she calmly advised us both: "Okay, but you must wash it first." Then she stretched out her hand.

There are many similar stories about our Rivka, and to now see her out of control and disoriented was too much for anyone to ignore. Something made Rivka look up lice online, and another miracle happened: *The lice fairy will take out lice for $90 guaranteed!* My husband, without checking out the company, approached me, gently kissed me on my forehead, and whispered, "Please take her today." We spent $290 plus the cost of products and then had three return visits costing $190 plus products—as well as two more visits costing $150. I'm thinking of going into that business and charging $50 plus products.

Now my Hadassa had lice. This time I treated my youngest daughter with the exact products that I'd bought and sat there for hours taking out nits—yes, live ones too. For those who have gone through a lice epidemic with your kids, you know what I went through. It was war! You have to attack the car, rugs, sheets, floors … everything. And it is worse than spring cleaning because the lice are microscopic. You have to clean everything *again* in three days.

CHAPTER II

I REMEMBER ANOTHER CRAZY MORNING, when the temperature in the house was about fifty degrees at ten in the morning (the weatherman called it June gloom). To avoid feeling guilty heating the house when it was only me at home, I decided to put on layers of clothes. Just as I put on my leggings, the phone rang. A familiar voice said, "Emah, open the door!"

I walked with the receiver in my hands and started screaming. To make a long story short, my daughter, all dolled up, had shown up from Florida unannounced and was giving me orders. She relieved me from all my duties of the day and started telling me what to wear. Out of a box came a golden brown fluffy gown with a crystal single-layered diamond crown with matching diamond shoes and then … Another ringing of the doorbell? Who could it be?

A strange-looking person walked in with a hatbox and a huge makeup box. Shoshana invited the woman in, had her set up in my den, and then proceeded to open the hatbox. I was in shock; she always knew how to fix my hair. I remember the day before her engagement party: she stole my black wig, and the next day, I saw it all puffed and curled, sitting in the hatbox, looking very distinguished. Now, after twenty years of my husband not letting me color my own hair, I gave in, I changed from wearing black haired wigs to my own color hair which is 80 percent white and the other black, so if some of my own hair sticks out of the wig it would blend better. She fixed my salt-and-pepper wig, styling it off my face, and added the special silver crystal crown to match.

I wanted an explanation. I demanded to know why two people were fussing over me and fixing me up as if I were a doll. The woman painted my face and then insisted that I put on false eyelashes; I protested. Shoshana insisted and then said, "Just look in the mirror." As usual, she was right. I had to agree that my eyes looked like I was twenty again.

Without so much as an explanation, she escorted me to a limo. "Are you kidding me? Did you win the lottery? What's going on?" I had not been in a white limo since the day I'd married David. On the way to the hall, I'd had my five little ones cooing and oohing the whole way, while Ruth, my best friend at the time, took pictures. After the happiest day of my life, David escorted me into the limo and held my hand the entire way. The ride was peaceful, with David on my right and the midnight moon on my left. The moon looked happy to me, and we both got a second chance.

You see, when G-d created the sun and moon on the fourth day, the moon complained, "How can there be two kings in one sky?" So G-d got angry and, as a result, made the moon smaller. The moon did repent, and G-d saw that the moon was sad and lonely so he gave him bright stars that would join him each night. David and I had been married for nine and a half years, and we were desperately struggling to make it work, especially for the children's sake. There was no turning back. That day, I felt like the moon—David and I got a second chance!

Shoshana snapped her fingers and woke me from my daydream. She then opened the door to the limo, and I hesitantly crouched in. "Shoshana, it's not my birthday yet! Does Daddy know about this?" She did not say a word. Something was going on, and she was not cracking, just smirking. It was only three in the afternoon when the limo pulled in front of the magnificent *Queen Mary*. This royal liner is bigger than the *Titanic*, traveled 1,001 times across the North Atlantic Ocean, and finally retired in Long Beach, California. What a dream boat. One of my daughters got married on this ship. I kept questioning her. "But why I'm here now?" She would not answer.

As I walked down the stairs to the banquet hall, I felt like Cinderella. The doors opened, and the band played a tune I'm never tired of hearing: the theme from *Hawaii Five-O*. What was happening? I could see enormous stand of white roses in the shape of a six and a zero. But I wasn't turning sixty until … I heard everyone scream "Surprise!" Did they make a mistake?

Staring at the crowd six feet ahead of me, I couldn't make out who was out there because of all the bright lights. My eyes were wet, and tears were running down my cheeks. I had no Kleenex, and I would feel embarrassed wiping my eyes with the palms of my hands. I remember my daddy saying compassionately, "Yael can cry forever; she has a whole ocean in her head." He was right.

Chapter III

My daughter sat me at the head table with many familiar faces, including relatives. I did not understand. I tried to look through my watery eyes, and standing beside me was a girl with an LBD (little black dress). With all the commotion I did not pay attention to how gorgeous she looked. I recognized it immediately and knew she'd gotten it at Nordstrom. It was puffy with an elegant trail of ruffles running like train tracks up and down and overlapping. The dress looked elegant. I Hope she will end up keeping the dress. She could never afford to buy herself a special dress. That's Shoshana for you.

She is five feet one and a bit shy of weighing ninety-eight pounds. She is my third child and second girl. How could I have had three children fourteen months apart? Almost breakdown time. Shoshana was valedictorian, finished a year of college, got a great job in the Diamond District, and now she has a bit of a challenge. I remember like it was yesterday when she moved to Florida, and just her luck, three weeks before moving into a twenty-three-hundred-square-foot house with a pool, her husband got laid off. She teaches kindergarten and subs, and she is struggling on her own full-time paycheck. She is truly wasting her time, for she is brilliant and could teach older kids, and she would feel so fulfilled, but she does not have the time to prepare lesson plans, or so she says. I remember her calling me one morning:

"Emah, I got it. I got it."

"Got what?" I asked.

"It came—it finally came."

Remembering what she was talking about (grant for college) I started to scream as if I had won the lottery. I continued jumping up and down and congratulating Shoshana, only when I listened to the other side of the line, I heard uncontrollable bawling. "Shoshana, what's the matter? You've been waiting for this for over a year, and you finally got it."

"Emah," she paused and took a break from her outburst, "There are not enough hours in a day; I have to sacrifice my husband and children that is huge."

"Shoshana listen, the most successful people are the busiest. No pain no gain."

I know she had a tough decision to make.

I was surprised one day when she called me on a Friday afternoon; she'd found her front door opened. It took her thirty seconds to realize that someone had been in her house. The first thing she did was take her kids to the neighbor and then call the police. The reason I was surprised was back then when they were just starting out in their new environment, my poor Shoshana had little of value in her house. There were mattresses on the floor, piles of books against the wall, one dinette table, sinks that didn't drain, a pool too expensive to clean, and the list can go on. They took her brand-new laptop that her husband had just gotten her for her birthday, two computers, and a pearl and crushed diamond necklace. She had made chocolate chip cookies for lunches, and five of them were gone. The total loss was three thousand dollars. They had ransacked the house that they had just moved into a year earlier, but the most painful part for me was that she had to deal with it alone. Her husband was in London for a week; his family had a special get-together.

Rueven works hard. He got his rabbi degree and was a rabbi for over four years in Australia. Yes, Down Under and over twenty-eight hours to fly there. Try it with a three-month-old. I went to help Shoshana out when her first daughter was born—only three months after mine. Like a crazy nut, I packed one suitcase with diapers, one with towels and pots and pans, and of course, every bubby's (grandmother's) dream: lots and lots of cute outfits for the new addition. Because my little Hadassa was older, I took along another suitcase with practically brand-new hand-me-down clothes from her auntie! I know; can you imagine? It's like that famous joke: What's the difference between a Reformed, Conservative, and Orthodox wedding? In a Reformed one, the rabbi is pregnant; in a Conservative one, the bride is pregnant; and in the Orthodox one, the mother of the bride is pregnant.

She and I breast-fed and walked with our babies together. Being in Australia was extremely relaxing. It was like America in the fifties. They have palm trees, amazing gardens, and great beaches. Most of the one-story building where my daughter lived was well maintained.

Rueven's shul (house of prayer) was the oldest shul in Australia, about one hundred years old, with all original rich mahogany wood. It could hold fourteen hundred people or more. The women were upstairs. Downstairs they would read the Torah (the Jewish Bible) and the rabbi would give speeches. I cooked two Friday night dinners for them, and for the last one, we invited the whole shul to come for a feast at the rabbi's house. Rueven was great with his congregation of about thirty-five people, who were mostly young Israelis. That was Rueven's life before Shoshana and his newborn.

Shortly after the second pregnancy, Shoshana decided to move back home. I see Reven works with restoring old Torahs he likes his work but he does not have much time with the kids, often he is called to work on Sunday.

Everyone seems to be suffering in this unstable economy. Shoshana, of course, would never ask for help. I begged her to take from the program for struggling families. The program some communities have is called "Tomchei Shabbos." Every Thursday night, you get an anonymous knock on the door, usually around seven thirty. When you open the door, you will find a sealed box. Twenty-two years ago, I was in a desperate situation, and I received packages like that. After cutting the tape off the first box, I discovered that it contained two bottles of milk, three pounds of ground beef, one cut-up chicken, and one loaf of bread. Experiencing that for the first time, I choked up and started moaning like a cow, hoping the kids would not hear me. I called the rabbi and demanded that he come pick up the box. He promised that he would take me off the list and not send one again. He lied! The second time, I convincingly explained that under no circumstances would I take that box of charity, and not only that, but it was on his head for wasting food. Then he promised *again* not to send me any food if only I took it in for the last time, and with a heavy heart, I did.

I tried to teach Shoshana that I was wrong in letting my kids feel hungry. Back then, I would rather them eat sandwiches made of margarine and sugar for their lunches and biscuits dipped in tea for supper than take any kind of handout. But like mother, like daughter, she follows suit. Now here she is, glowing with pride. I have confidence that the wheel of fortune will change.

I know G-d does not like fractions; when two people find each other, the two halves become a whole. And one thing I know for sure is that Rueven loves Shoshana. They are whole together, and he knew after the first date. He went home, called his best friend, and told him, "I'm going to marry her."

Because they live so far away and we don't see them often, I insist that they come for Passover. The last time they came, their three-year-old son, Mendy, ran in, twisting from side to side and holding on to his private parts. "I have to make!" he shouted. "I can't make it in that bathroom; the toilet is pink. It's for girls." That gave us a laugh that we will never forget.

Now Shoshana proudly hands me a trophy shaped like a heart … She rattles a sentence in Yiddish and then translates in English: "My mother gives from the bottom of her heart with endless bounces. Emah! Stand up and take your first due award." A photographer had shot a picture while Shoshana was speaking. I give her a hug and a big kiss on her cheek. I whisper in her ear that if it were up to me, I would be giving her the award for having the biggest heart in the world. This girl, more so than any of my other children, will go out of her way to help anyone, no matter what she is doing or how it inconveniences her and Rueven. I remind her how she used her babysitting money to buy Shabbat shoes for one of her friends, and how, without permission, she gave one of her uniform skirts to the same friend to keep.

Just as both of us take our seats, I hear a voice behind me: "Don't get too comfortable." It's my oldest child. Now what in the world is he up to? I imagine that this is going to be my birthday roast a whole two months early.

Chapter IV

Taking the microphone, he adjusts it a bit higher. He repeats his words as he looks at me: "Emah, don't get too comfortable. I'm next."

I could never mistake this boy for anyone else; there is only one Shimon, and he is tall, dark, and handsome. When he was fourteen, we took a trip to Sacramento with nine kids. Our first time there, we'd driven ten hours. I was pregnant with number seven, and we'd taken the scenic route. We'd stopped at the aquarium and had our own homemade kosher breakfast at the Ramada Inn Gardens. This time, because tickets were cheap, we opted to fly. However, the flight there was delayed for hours. The kids walked up and down, and I can't even remember how they entertained themselves, but we managed.

We traveled all over San Francisco, going on famous bridges and spending a wonderful Shabbat with my husband's first brother, who owns a four-acre house with a swimming pool. The kids, having been overdosed with love, were all in a happy and playful mood as we boarded the aircraft for the flight back. Each one found their own seats; the older child took a smaller one and looked after him or her the whole flight. I, of course, had the youngest between my husband and me, and I had an aisle seat.

As I got ready to buckle my seat belt, I spotted Shimon sitting one row up and on the aisle seat opposite mine. Before we took off, I decided to cause some mischief. I pounced on him and tickled him under his right arm. The person occupying that seat was not my oldest son! I jumped up and profusely apologized, trying to wipe away whatever sweat was on my hand. Like a broken record, I screamed repeatedly, "I thought you were my oldest son! He has the same short-sleeved shirt as you, and you look ..." By that time, everyone was standing, and Shimon popped his head up from four rows ahead of us. "See! See! See! Look, there he is; he looks just like you—same shirt, and from the back, same short haircut." I was so embarrassed, and my kids and husband were laughing so hard that I could see some of their back molars. Shimon proudly smiled as if he'd planned this whole purely accidental case of mistaken identity.

As the oldest of the first five kids, Shimon had to grow up fast. I remember one Sunday when he insisted that he had to go for a walk and said he would be back in an hour. We lived five streets from the famous Sunset Boulevard and two streets above Melrose. There was no way on this earth that I'd let my child walk alone in this neighborhood. I offered to drive him, but he refused and just continued pleading, changing his request to a half-hour walk. Something inside me weakened, and I allowed him to go, but only if he came back in exactly thirty minutes. We both checked our watches, and like a jet plane, he took off around the corner.

It was Sunday, so I busied myself with laundry and dishes. I think I must have looked at the oven clock a hundred times. Just as I was about to walk out my front door, I could see from the corner of my eye that he was back, carrying this huge monster of a plant. As I looked closer, I said, "Shimon what is this? What are you doing? Why did you not let me drive you?" I kept repeating my questions.

My Shimon caught his breath and finally answered me. "It's Mother's Day today, and I wanted it to be a surprise. We all chipped in. Daddy gave the most, and I got you your very first white rose bush." (The kids call my husband Daddy out of respect and love for him, even though he is their stepfather.)

"What? I'm so surprised! I would have given you longer to get it. You must have run the whole mile back and forth." Shimon was so proud of himself when we all planted the bush.

That boy could do no wrong, and I was proud of him. When he was only five years old, his rabbi gave everyone fake money to buy toys, candy, and books. Shimon saved for six months, and the day of his birthday, he got his first Torah (the first five books of the Hebrew Bible). Each book was only four inches wide and two inches thick, and he was so proud of them. He kept them with all his special things and even took them with him when he got married and had his own home. Today he is thirty-seven, and he still cherishes them.

I watch him now as he talks. Why is he holding an airplane in his hand? Oh no! Here he goes. He is going to tell his versions of all my mishaps with flying. From my point of view, one of them was a nightmare that would last a lifetime.

It was a week before Shimon's wedding. He had gone out with a few girls from Australia before he finally committed. When Shimon got his rabbi degree from Sydney, the director, knowing his potential, did not want to lose him. He took on the role of matchmaker and came up with a few candidates.

Ironically, the first girl was a child I'd taught in kindergarten twenty years earlier when her family lived in California. She came from a dysfunctional blended family of fourteen. She was from the second batch of kids, and her name was Irene. Out of ten months of school with five days a week, she attended maybe two days a week, and that was with loud hollering and crying that lasted for thirty minutes, until the mother decided she'd had enough. She was a sight to see: nose running down her lips, unkempt hair, and clothes that were five times bigger than her petite size. Without any sympathy, I roared at Shimon and absolutely refused to let him date that girl. Without my blessing, Shimon insisted on going out with Miss Irene. I called the head rabbi of the town and voiced my opinion about the family and *that girl*! The rabbi assured me that he had seen her in New York and said that she was put together nicely. He also reminded me that Shimon would not be marrying the family but the girl. After a week of dating, my Shimon informed me that he was falling head over heels for a girl I totally disapproved of.

When my phone rang on a Thursday, I almost couldn't recognize the voice. "Who is this?" I waited a little and continued after hearing a little sob. "Shimon, is that you?" He concurred that it was. My Shimon was brokenhearted! Miss Irene wanted to go slow; she was not sure if Shimon was right for her. I wanted to tell him "I told you so," but instead I asked for all the grim details and suggested that he call her before Shabbat and wish her a good Shabbat. He pointed out that they both know Rabbi Freedman and were invited separately to a Saturday night party for a three-year-old's cutting of the hair for the first time. Shimon did not want to go. I exploded. "Are you kidding me? You've known the rabbi for four years, all through your schooling, and you're not going to show up because of a disoriented lunatic who is paranoid and screwy wacko, and who will never know what is good for her even if it's right in front of her eyes. *You listen to me!*" I demanded. "I want you to buy one rose, and at the party, go up to her, have her sit down, and say, 'Listen, it was nice, but I think that you are not for me.' Drop the rose on her lap like an atomic bomb." My son complied, and he was soon on a plane to Melbourne to meet a very rich girl.

Shimon called regularly to report on his interactions and experiences with her. Her hair was down and frizzy with knots the first time they went out, and she wore a gaudy-looking wristwatch and high heels. Her outfit could not reveal if she is a size sixteen or six. The second time, Shimon, loving water sports, let her know they were going boating, and she showed up in higher heels, mini skirt exposing her fat thighs, with the same watch and same hairstyle. By the third time, Shimon could not look at her unkempt appearance any more. She just turned my son off.

The third girl, Rachi Farkash from Israel, was very honest. She passionately explained to Shimon that her best friend, Ruthy, who was in the same seminary (girls' school) with her, was the perfect girl for him. When Shimon asked where she was from, he was informed that she was from England. Great! Now we had to get involved with a cold, snobby British girl.

Shimon asked Rachi, their matchmaker, to have the girl meet him in Long Beach, California, because he was heading home for good. To our surprise, Ruthy had agreed to stay with a Rabbi Green. His wife, Rose, was originally from England (she was Hadassah's second grade teacher), and Ruthy's mother, Rachel, knows Rose's mother, who still lives in London. They work to put together monthly women's functions for about one to two hundred people.

To make a long story short, they met in the airport for the first time. Shimon was to wear his black hat and jacket, and he opted to hold one red rose. Ruthy was going to spot Shimon. I remember my son saying how nerve-racking it was when he saw a girl that wasn't to his liking. He would wish under his breath, "Please, G-d, don't let that be her. Please no! No! No!" He did that a few times, until finally this bombshell appeared. She was five feet ten and had short, straight black hair and a white complexion. And even today, she looks like she could be a real model. I think she looks like Snow White.

Straight from the airport, Shimon took her out to Shore Line Village and kept her well into the night before she first walked into her host house in Long Beach. The next day, he took her to Los Angeles, and they walked the pier. He also took her to Pat's, an exclusive restaurant. That night was a Friday, and just before sunset, he had to bring her back before candle lighting time. The next day was Shabbat, and both came to shul to pray. Shimon sent his two younger sisters to say hello to Ruthy on the women's side of the shul. After eating lunch at separate locations, they met and walked around again until sunset.

Now comes the killer part! After Shabbat was over, Shimon took a shower, got dressed, and was ready to go out and hit the town. Ruthy said, "I want to take a break tonight." He got the same medicine he'd dished out to that Irene girl. That's all she said, and my Shimon's heart stopped beating for a few seconds. He came home depressed and called my favorite cousin, Josef. Josef is always good with the kids. He plays soccer and Stratego with them.

To make his downhearted cousin feel good, Josef took him out bowling and for a drink.

The next day was Sunday, and as usual, I was cleaning the house. Through the window I saw my son on the patio swing. I armed myself with a turkey, lettuce, and tomato sandwich in one hand and the portable phone in the other. "Okay!" I said, approaching him. "She never said not to call her, so come on—go ahead and eat something and call her." With that, I left. Half an hour later, I passed by the window, and my son was alive again, laughing and gesturing with his hands that everything was *great*. I could see that the sandwich was untouched, but that was okay; we were back in business again. I did a little jig and clapped my hands, singing, "By George, she got it. She got it! The rain in Spain falls mainly on the plain—and where does it rain? In the plain ..." And off I went, crazy as ever.

Apparently, Ruthy had asked to take a break because she had not had a chance to call her parents in England, because of the time difference, to let them know how things were going between them.

That Monday was a big day. I was packing for that trip to Australia with my three-month-old. I had two hours to get to the airport.

The phone rang. It was Shimon. "Oh my G-d. What's wrong? You just left fifteen minutes ago. Why are you calling? Did she end it?"

"No, no, Emah. I told her you are going to Australia, and I want her to meet you."

"Meet me now? Why? Oh, Shimon, I'm not dressed." The phone went dead. The doorbell rang not even five minutes later. I grabbed my wig and ran to open the door, only to notice that I did not have my shoes on.

"Hello," I said.

"Hello," she responded with a perfect smile, Shimon by her side.

"I'm Shimon's mom. Come in. I am so sorry; I'm in a bit of a rush."

"It's okay. I've been in your house before." She spoke with her hands in the pockets of her overcoat. I was in shock and did not open my mouth.

"I came last summer," she continued. "You hosted the dinners many times for the girl counselors."

"And we walked you home—now I remember," I added.

"I saw Shimon's picture on your wall."

I knew that she must have seen Sophie's bat mitzvah family portrait in the living room. I kissed her hard on the cheek, and then I kissed her again, and as they were leaving, I yelled, "I love you!"

Without missing a beat, Shimon yelled back with great enthusiasm, "Hey, that's my job! I have to say I love you."

With warmth in my heart, I responded, "Yes, but I said it first."

Plans were made to meet me in Australia and let Ruthy be exposed to her, G-d willing, new surroundings. Shimon grew up in California, but he is in Australia during the year teaching. The gathering was on a Sunday, and to my son's surprise, there was ample food. He showed up with ten different dips because he did not trust me. I was introduced to her mom, who was from Indonesia, and her father, a dentist. That explained the straight teeth and perfect smile. He was born in South Africa, but he could not leave England because of his business and ten children.

Before you knew it, arrangements were made for the big day. I had two married daughters but had no idea what to expect when marrying off a son. My first daughter cost my husband and me twenty thousand dollars, and I had nothing to eat but two hot dogs in blankets, which Josef stuffed in my mouth while we were taking pictures. The food had run out about an hour into the wedding party. The second daughter's wedding cost twenty-eight thousand dollars, and there was no water to drink, not one pitcher on anyone's table. The caterer had forgotten all about the drinks. Now here we were.

We paid for Shoshana and Rueven to fly in from Australia with a three-month-old. We paid for Devorah and Eli to fly in from Israel with their two-year-old, and we were taking six more kids: one fifteen and the others ten and under. One of our daughters, Sophie, who is David's daughter from his first marriage, is only six months older than Pennina. She couldn't come because she was attending the University of New York art and theater school and had a big performance and a final exam that she could not miss. This wedding had so far cost us twenty-five thousand dollars.

My son explained that he was going to New York on Friday; he wanted to pray that weekend at the holy shul with the rebbe at Seven-Seventy in Crown Heights. Not knowing anyone in New York, Shimon arranged to have Friday night dinner with us. We ate together but mostly slept in separate places. I had my infant and two boys; Pennina and the two girls were together. Shabbat morning I ran to Seven-Seventy, hoping to see my son called to read the Torah (he is a Levi, and a Levi is always called second to read from the Torah). I knew by all the commotion that either I had come too late or he'd gone to a different room to pray. Anyway, I was jealous. That afternoon, my oldest would not be eating with me. He was to be with his father, my ex, and then together they would fly to England.

Giving birth to the first five kids, it was hard for me to share them with someone I felt absolutely nothing toward. The reason for the breaking up of a family could be any of the three *A*s: adultery, addiction, and/or abuse. How about he or she is lazy never working enough days to bring home one paycheck; how about plain old selfish—only thinking of number one, himself. I had chosen him immaturely, thinking that I could change him. But the reason someone gets divorced doesn't matter. The side effects do. I got rid of the cancer, but the children are still subjected to being tennis balls, tossed around from one side of the court to the other. Even though I was only going to miss my firstborn son for one afternoon, the thought of the ex having him started me thinking bad thoughts. I wished that the ex would not show up to the wedding—that maybe, with some luck, he would miss the plane.

That night, after a wonderful Shabbat, we packed our luggage and drove to the airport with ample time to spare. That's when my nightmare started.

We approached the ticket agent. I plopped down six kids' passports and handed her mine. She gave a big sigh and continued looking at me, authenticating my picture. She continued to check the kids' documents, looking as if she were doing the tango or mambo with the upper part of her body. She slam-dunked one … two … and three passports down in front of my face and almost stingingly said, "Well, they're not going anywhere!" She was black and had a thick Brooklyn accent, and she was hard to understand.

"Who …? Why …?" I was gasping for air.

"Their passports are expired," she bellowed loudly, starting to shuffle papers. "Only you and the other three can go."

"No! No!" I protested. "That can't be."

Seeing me panic, she tried to help. "I can book you on a six o'clock flight for tomorrow morning." Annoyingly, both of us simultaneously whispered that there were no immigration offices open on Sunday. Her attitude changed when I informed her that I was the mother of the groom, and that the wedding was taking place on Tuesday afternoon. She charged me a changing fee of seven hundred dollars and got me on the latest flight on Monday, at six thirty. As a bonus, she looked up the address of the immigration building in Manhattan and affectionately spoke under her breath, advising me to get there before it opened the next morning.

By then, I could feel that my face was all wet; tears were racing past my cheeks and down my neck. I could not even think of what to do next. I looked at the frightful mess around me: seven unmatched, deformed suitcases, a huge fold-up stroller, backpacks—not to mention five human beings that acted as if someone had come by and slapped each of them. Oh, yes, time to nurse my six-month-old—no time for an outpouring of sympathy now. It felt as if someone had just died, all of us abandoned the airport. No one said a word. I dove into my purse and tried to find my cell phone.

Yoni was an Israeli that we hooked up with from Union Taxi, and he also had a Jewish-run shuttle. He had picked us up at just before six in the morning on Friday when we arrived in New York; and at nine thirty on Saturday night, just an hour before, he had brought us to the airport to depart. With no explanation, I called him en route to turn around and please pick us up. He was about to retire for the night, but making ninety dollars each trip, he could not pass it up. We had to have a large van for seven people and all our belongings. Yoni showed up at eleven o'clock. "Ma kara?" he growled in my native tongue, asking me what had happened.

My lips felt glued shut, and gone was my smile and wedding cheer and enthusiasm. New tears started accompanying my voice, and with few words, I shamefully explained that I didn't check all the kids' passports. Yoni handed me the tissue box and continued talking in my native tongue.

"Where is your husband?" Not hearing a response, he continued bashing my David. "He should be with you. Who goes traveling alone with six kids ... and with an infant yet? You are a strong, beautiful woman. He should be proud of you; he takes it easy, and you have to deal with their welfare every second. I know—I come from a large family, and I have total respect for you. If I were you ..."

I had to make him stop. He did not understand. For forty-five minutes, I explained how my only true love is David. I am what I am today because of my husband. He treats me like a queen. David married me with five kids under ten; we are a blended family (my five plus David's one from before, and then we had five more kids together). We have eleven kids, four boys and seven girls. So far, David has paid for six weddings for five kids (yes, one got divorced after two weeks); ten circumcision parties; four bar mitzvahs, plus buying their tefillin (religious wear for men); and six bat mitzvahs. Moreover, he takes the family on two annual vacations (once after tax season and Pesach break, and once in the winter for Chanukah). Whenever the kids need a cosigner or to borrow money, which some still haven't paid back, David gives openly. He treats all the kids the same; no one gets special treatment. In my David's eyes, they're all equal.

I worked like a dog back in the day. I never knew what it was like to be a real mother or a wife. With the last five kids, however, I was home for each one of them. Supper was always on the table the minute they came home from school, the cooking done with flair. My nights were enjoyable, the *best ever.*

After all that, I explained to Yoni that it was tax season and David couldn't take much time off work. He was going to England on Sunday from Los Angeles and turning around and coming back on Wednesday. All this just so we can have clothes, food, and a roof over our heads.

We parted, agreeing to meet again Monday morning at six thirty. It was midnight, and we had to go to our hosts and break the news that we had to stay another two nights. I didn't know how I would call David in Europe. He would be waiting anxiously at the airport to pick us up. The phone at our host's house was blocked, and I could not make international phone calls. I called my cousin in Queens, New York, and I lucked out when her ten-year-old son picked up. I desperately asked him to call England and forward the information. At that point, I couldn't care less if he got all the numbers or not.

With that done, I fell on my pillow quietly and started bawling nonstop. No one was around to comfort me. I cried bitterly and in my head asked, *Why? Why? I'm going to miss my son's wedding. I gave birth to him. I taught him how to read and write, and he struggled with memorizing the Chomash (Bible).*

I would say that Shimon turned out okay. Still, I felt I was being punished. There's a good reason for everything that happens, and nothing that G-d does is bad—so I have learned. It just takes time. Sometimes you learn why things turn out the way they do, and sometimes you will never know.

I turned my wet pillow over, just to repeat the exact same thing on the other side. I felt as if I had a bad hangover. Feeling I had no choice, I took two Tylenol PM tablets and forced myself to sleep.

Sunday was sunny, and there was snow on the ground. I love Sundays because they are a nothing day, just as the song "Manic Monday" goes. I totally relate to that crazy week schedule—cooking, cleaning, homework, baths, and so on.

My Pennina had not said a word. She never even argued that since her passport was okay, she could go alone. After all, she was fifteen. I grabbed her cheeks, kissed them hard, and promised her that she would not miss her brother's wedding. I told her that if I (and the rest of the clan) couldn't join her, she might go alone with Yaacove, my then three-year-old. She smiled and returned my kiss, giving me a big hug as well.

I announced to everyone that after we prayed at Seven-Seventy, we were all going out for breakfast: hot chocolate and doughnuts. For some reason, my five-year-old son, Alvin, did not understand the severity of the situation, and he was fooling around while saying *Tehillim* (Psalms). I ignored him. After a great breakfast, we went to Union Taxi Service. I had used a credit card to pay for the shuttle the night before and to prepay for the Manhattan trip the next day. I only had thirty dollars in cash. This wedding was getting expensive. I had no choice but to add everything we needed to my Citibank MasterCard.

Even though the sun was out, it was deceiving, for the temperature was thirty degrees. We'd had to walk from the house to Seven-Seventy, from Seven-Seventy to Fast Bagel, from Fast Bagel to Union Taxi, and now we had to find a store that carried kosher formula without milk for the baby since I would not be able to attend to her needs most of the next day. From the kosher warehouse to a children's museum, everything was in a one-mile radius, but having my six flesh and blood children walking in the chilly air was sickening to me. I spent one hundred dollars, and we were set at the museum for a good four hours or more. That place was my heaven on earth. Every floor had a different exhibit. There was even miniature golf on the roof. There were ten holes, and each hole was a mitzvah (kind deed) that you could do. There was a miniature kitchen where you could actually get a cholent recipe (a dish I make with barley, meat, and potatoes—no beans). You can set the table with colorful plastic plates and cutlery. There was even a place to go shopping with a tiny shopping cart, and the "store" contained everything you could find at Ralphs—and more. There was cauliflower, chicken, ketchup … although everything was fake and made of plastic. We saw ambulances and fire trucks that the kids got to go on. The basement had a movie theater, and they put on a show about Pharaoh and Moshe.

It was getting close to five o'clock. Where to go for supper? As we were coming out of the elevator, we saw a restaurant. Great. It beat walking in the cold weather. Out came my charge card, and *plop* went the bill, adding another seventy-five dollars just for burgers, soup, and salad. We spoke about the next day, and I told Pennina that she had to be at the apartment from six fifteen on with Yaacove, age three, and my six-month-old baby Hadassa. She was capable, and she would need to stay by the phone. If everything worked out, she would have to call the taxi and meet us at the immigration office.

Remembering that dark day in my life, I suddenly pick my head up, and to my surprise, everyone is laughing with Shimon. Shimon has just asked a question: "How many of you think that (a) my mother should go only with three kids; (b) she should give up the whole thing; or (c) she should just let Pennia go alone."

Looking out at this banquet of at least one hundred people, I admire the elegant black-and-white tablecloths and notice that even the chairs have skirts. I see my favorite long-stemmed white roses. I can't believe it; I'm sitting onstage on the *Queen Mary*, laughing at their answers: 68 percent said that I should turn around and go home; 15 percent said to just send Pennia; 17 percent were sure I should go to the wedding and make arrangements for the other three kids. That thought had never crossed my mind—never would I abandon my children. As Shimon continues his story, my thoughts go back to that Manic Monday.

At five thirty, I got up gingerly so I wouldn't wake Hadassa. I said my morning prayers and got my Alvin up. I made him tea and honey and waited for Pennia to arrive with her two younger siblings. Everything went according to plan. The baby was still asleep, and she would get her first feeding at six thirty as well as every four hours after that, with fruit and vegetables for lunch.

Yoni was on time, and I helped Miriam, Rivka, and Alvin into the backseat, taking the front myself. Off we went. Yoni, as with most Israelis, was very optimistic, but right then he was giving me a massive headache, although I know he meant well. He was so sweet, saying he had never prayed so hard in his life for anyone as he did for all of us to go b'shalom (with peace) and come back b'shalom (with peace). I looked at my watch. Okay, if he prayed, he must have had to get up a bit earlier.

You're never supposed to mistrust a Jew; you should always think of him as good. But look what happened with Madoff; he financially killed everyone that was ever involved with him—over thirty billion dollars he embezzled. I'm only accustomed to seeing one-hundred-dollar bills when I have to pay by cash, when I'm late with my electric bill and so forth. What is thirty billion dollars? How does someone do that? People like Madoff must not be able to sleep well at night.

I thanked Yoni for his prayers. He knew to wait for my daughter's phone call, and he said he would try his best. We got out into the cold weather and zipped into the building. We opened the double heavy doors, and I felt the comfortable warm heat inside. The foyer was large, and after taking three wide steps, we faced the elevators. I tried to press the button, but the guard stopped me and asked the famous question: "Do you have an appointment?"

"No," I answered nervously.

"Okay. The offices don't open until nine o'clock." As I started backing up, this black six-foot guard said, "You can't wait here!"

I asked the obvious question: "Why?"

He explained to me that since 9/11, no one was allowed to congregate together in any government buildings.

"Thanks," I answered, and into the twenty-three-degree weather we went. The color white dominated the scene around us. Snow was gently falling, and normally it would be so romantic, clean, and fun—now it was our enemy! Alvin stood behind me; I felt his body glued to mine. Rivka was crying and holding my hand, and Miriam angrily stood two feet away from me, as if she wanted nothing to do with me. I couldn't blame her. I cupped my hand over the side of her face and smiled, pulling her next to my vacant side. As I wasn't wearing gloves, the tops of my hands were like steel wool due to being exposed to such cold weather. We had no boots; I'm sure the kids' feet were freezing.

Five minutes passed, and we were in the building again—this time not by the elevators but by shiny rows of black phones. I picked up the phone, and to no surprise, it was automated. "Please spell your name and then enter your social security number." I panicked. Opening my purse, I remembered emptying it because there was so much stuff to think of, like seven passports, a pacifier, diapers, and so forth, that I did not want to take all my credit cards. I'd taken out my Discover, American Express, Chase Visa, Sears, Gap, Ralphs, Costco, Smart & Final card … and my social security card. I'd told myself that I would not need any of them, just my driver's license and the kids' passports. *Wrong! Wrong! Wrong!* How wrong I was.

I would try the phone again. This time, I took off my layers of clothes, put down my purse, and demanded that Miriam look after the stuff. I whispered a thanks and sent a kiss her way. I picked the phone up and spelled my name. When it asked for my social security number, I exclaimed, "I don't have it!" The third time I tried, I pounded the phone like a hammer onto the receiver at least a few times. Then, without thinking, I hollered like a lion, "*I do not have my damn social security number!*" Looking around, I noticed a boy of about fifteen and an older Russian couple dressed in heavy long winter coats. The woman was holding shopping bags made out of cloth. My head felt heavy, and with no control, I felt myself going down headfirst. I could hear Miriam screaming *Emah!* Then, to my surprise, my body was caught before I hit the cold white marble floor. I felt two strong hands grab me and bring me up to eye level.

"Listen, I heard what you said. My parents do not have social security numbers, and they too need their passports for tomorrow." Removing myself from his grip, I slowly informed him that I needed new passports today. I also informed him that I have tried to talk to someone alive on the phone but it is impossible; it's only a machine. He promised to get me an appointment. While he and Miriam went on their mission, the other two kids and I sat on the floor, and only then could I start breathing normally. I saw Miriam blushing as she walked next to the nice-looking teenager, except that I was mistaken. He was no teenager! I found out later that he was twenty-two. He returned shortly and reported, "Okay, you have a ten o'clock appointment."

"Thank G-d," I said.

"No," was his answer. "My name is David."

Oh my gosh, all my angels that come help me, whether I'm in my hour of distress or not, are named David. My computer guy, my handyman, my banker, some of my doctors, and of course, my knight in shining armor, my true and only lover, my friend, my partner in life is my husband David.

Looking down at my silver watch with two tiny diamonds, I saw that it was 9:36 a.m. We had time to kill again! We bundled up and marched out of the building, only to discover a liquor store around the corner. There, I comforted the kids with two packs of potato chips to share and a hot tea with honey. The owner of the business, who happened to be from India, my parents' homeland, gave me a hard time and insisted that I pay sixty-five cents for an additional three empty hot cups. To him, my kids must have looked like they would shoplift from his store, so we could not find a safe haven in his place. Out into the cold we went once more. I was relieved to find that it was five to ten.

Back into failure territory, this time full speed ahead, we headed to the elevator to travel up to the fifteenth floor. Of course, the youngest always yelled, "It's my turn to push the button!" But this time, two must have felt my stress and been scared, for they would not open their mouths unless spoken to. But not Alvin! He asked, "Where's number thirteen?"

Immediately, I had to stop thinking of my world and force myself to come down to his. "The number thirteen is bad luck for the rest of the nations of the world, except not for the Jews. There was a tyrant by the name of Haman, and he hated the Jews, so he decided to annihilate all the chosen people from all over the world because he was jealous. He picked the thirteen of Adar."

Excitedly, my son yelled, "Purim!" (In March, it's the happiest holiday in the Jewish calendar.)

"Yes, that's right. Haman saw that there were no Jewish holidays on that month. He did not realize that our leader and rabbi, Moshe, was born and passed away on the seventh of March. So a *big* miracle happened on the thirteenth of March. After the Jews fasted for three days and prayed, King Achesverose changed the decree, listening to his queen, Esther, who happened to be Jewish, and had the evil Jew hater hung, along with all his ten sons, and the Jews got permission to defend themselves against any other attacks from his followers. That's why we get to celebrate Purim!"

The whole time I was explaining this to my son, I made sure to keep eye contact. My cousin from Jerusalem told me that a woman with cancer once went to a rabbi in the city to get a blessing for a speedy recovery. Strangely, he'd asked her, "Do you look at your children when they require your attention, like when you're answering their questions?" Her answer was, "No, I'm usually doing things." The rabbi insisted that she must look into the children's eyes when she spoke to them. This conversation had made me relax and build my confidence; I needed it for what was to come next.

The elevator opened right in front of the office, which looked like a bank. There were twelve windows, and not surprisingly, only three were open. I wonder why that is. Everywhere you went, it could be nine o'clock sharp, and never would you see all the tellers working at the same time. Never in a supermarket, bank, post office, or any other office. I believe they have the other windows just for show. I think there should be a law that during working hours, every window must be mandatorily opened. But that's a different fight for another time.

Our number was twenty-six. Even though we had an appointment, we still had to take a number; we took our seats among sixty or more foreigners. As I looked around, I felt the comfort of carpet under my shoes, and I liked the soft blue walls all around me. Now I needed a big miracle.

I got the children to follow me, saying by heart, Tehillim 121, my father's favorite psalm. The first time he said it was when my mom did not come home with my new brother from the hospital. Before putting us to bed for the night, he said this special Tehillim. He sang it so passionately, with his eyes closed, and it was such a beautiful tune that I still remember it to this day. That day, my kids and I said it at least fifty times, and then, to my astonishment, our number was called. Only ten minutes had passed.

I approached the counter, and a youngish stocky worker moved her red painted lips, asking, "Can I help you?"

"I have to renew the passports for these three; we have to catch a flight to London at six thirty tonight."

"Do you have their social security numbers and birth certificates?"

"No!"

"Then I can't help you."

"Listen, I'm the mother of the groom, and these too are my children. Look, they have the same last names, and here are their old passports. You can check that they are citizens of America and everything. Please … it's my son's wedding tomorrow." Everything I'd just said was ignored.

"I can't give you new passports unless you have their birth certificates and social security numbers. Sorry, I can't help you."

"You must!" I took a breath and then loudly and aggressively demanded, "I want to speak to a supervisor!"

Within seconds, my voice traveled through the whole office, and a sophisticated middle-aged black woman approached and asked what was going on. The worker explained that I had no social security numbers or birth certificates for the three children in question.

"I'm not from here. I live in Long Beach, California, and we just stopped over to spend the weekend with my son, the groom. He had to pray at the holy gravesides of our rabbis, and this was his last weekend single, so we were with him."

"Let me see your driver's license." Thank G-d I had that. I handed it to her. She looked at it and then calmly said, "Is there any way you can call home to get the social security numbers and certificates faxed to us?"

"No, my husband is in London; there is no one home."

The manager took over the counter, saying, "You need a letter from your husband that gives you permission to let you take his kids out of the country."

Before she could add another word, I yelped, "*What*!"

"Please do not scream. I'm trying to help you. Your husband must give you an affidavit; it's a document that must be notarized."

"How do I do that?" My voice was a bit too strong.

"There's a liquor store around the corner. He has a fax machine, and when you have that document, come back up."

"Do I need another appointment?"

"No, I'll take care of you."

As I turned around and went toward the kids, I heard, "The children each need passport pictures."

"Oh … no!" I hollered. "Where do I get those?" The holler turned into a screech, and all the tears started gushing out.

The one in charge was very sensitive; she motioned me to come back. "Listen," she said, putting her two hands on one of my arms. "It will work out. Go to the store. He has a fax machine and takes passport pictures, so you can do two things at once. Go quickly and I will help you."

"What's your name in case I come back and you're not here?"

"My name is Natasha. Good luck."

Without much fuss, the kids were bundled up and ready to go again. Alvin, on the other hand, protested, "I don't want to go out into the cold again." I apologized and helped him zip his zipper.

Back at the liquor store, the owner was not too happy to see us. After his last customer left, I questioned how much three passport pictures were and asked if I could please use his fax number so the affidavits would be sent here. The store owner charged me fifteen dollars per picture, and the use of the fax was thirty-five dollars. At this point, who cared what it cost? I proceeded to give him my Citibank MasterCard, and I asked how long it would take.

"About twenty-five minutes."

The four of us went to the street to locate a phone booth. Once we found one, the three little kids had to wait outside in the cold while I made a collect call to England the day before the wedding.

"I can't believe it. Is this normal?" The Kurtzmens were understanding; I found out later that they'd accepted many collect calls that day. Within five minutes, they located my husband.

"Hello?" said his familiar voice. "You poor thing. How are you managing?"

"David, I can't begin to explain. Just listen. The immigration office won't let me have passports until you fax me a notarized affidavit saying that you give permission for me to take all three kids to London. Can you also get their social security numbers?" My husband is a CPA, and his computer has all the information he needs.

"Okay, I love you, Yael. You can do this! Do you have any money?"

I explained that I had only twenty dollars left and was using my charge card, and then I added, "I love you more!"

I could not win the war against the coldness of the snow, so I decided to do the next best thing: beg!

Into the liquor store we went. "Please can we wait inside in the corner? The blizzard is turning my children into snowmen. Their cheeks are like ripe tomatoes. We are not from here—we don't have the proper clothes or boots. Would it be okay?" The man looked like I was about to pull something over his head. "Can we have two cups of tea with honey, please?" I continued. He came back with the pictures and four cups of tea. I was so pleased, although I'd known the pictures would be no good. They were the right size and all, but those did not look like the Goldmen faces I know. All three children had frightened looks. They were like mug shots, showing no emotion. As the storekeeper handed me the credit card, I asked his name.

"Raja," he answered proudly.

"That means king."

"Yes."

"My parents are from India," I continued. "My father's name was Kollatker; my mother's was Wrestler."

"My parents are from New Delhi," he added.

"Mine are from Bombay."

"Oh, yes, there was a big Jewish community there."

Before I could continue our research on our similar backgrounds, Alvin said he had to use the bathroom. Back at what seemed like our second home, into the immigration office we went. We then returned to the liquor store see if any papers had come. We got a negative sign from Raja. So we ventured out toward the phone booth, and I made another collect call. This time, I thought about the children, how they must miss talking to their dad. I got my husband on the phone.

"Sweetheart, what's with the affidavits?"

"We're working on it. We're trying to find an open notary."

Stiffly, I said, "Okay," and I handed the phone over to Miriam. After being calm this whole time, she took the phone and started crying.

"Daddy, pleeease sends the papers now! Are you going to do it or not? Do it now!" Miriam had come undone. After ending the call, I put her face to my chest, and we all walked around the block. The snowflakes felt refreshing on my skin, but I could barely open my eyes against the falling snow. Then we checked in with Raja. *Yes!* The notarized copies had come, and feeling some hope and enthusiasm, I dashed out of the store with them, racing to Natasha.

We entered the familiar office again, and Natasha was ready for us. She looked at the genuine certificates and said, "Do you have any other proof that these children are yours?"

I went frigid, my mouth pinching the bottom lip as if that would stop what was about to happen. My face tightened, and without warning, my brain just shattered. I started to cry aloud.

Natasha kept questioning me. "Do your kids go to school? There must be someone there who can testify that these are your children." My nose was running, and my face was wet. I could tell Natasha was trying to make out the words I said next.

"Lubavitch Hebrew School; Willow Lane; Westminster, California." I gave her the number, and Natasha handed me a box of tissue before going to the phone. I saw her talking to someone, and she was smiling as she came toward me. "Mrs. Goldmen, do you know Melanie?" I nodded my head. "She's the school director's secretary," she continued. "She is going to fax me, confirming that she knows you're the mother and David is the father—and also send me the social security numbers for each of them. With two papers showing proof of your children, we can process the passports. Do you have the pictures of the children?" I handed them over, and she asked me to have a seat. I looked at the watch and saw that it was noon. I said Tehillim to myself.

A few minutes passed, and Natasha called and waved to me to approach the window. She was holding a piece of paper with the letterhead from the Lubavitch Hebrew Academy School from Long Beach. The letter also showed the names of the board members, and David Goldmen was the first on that list. The dean of the school, Rabbi Levi Schustermen, had signed the letter stating that the children attended the school, and that David and Yael were their parents.

"Okay, Mrs. Goldmen, relax. You should have the passports by two thirty."

The catastrophe was over; we were almost home free. Now I looked at the children and hugged them tight. I sent them to the machine to buy a Coke to share. Alvin was happy he didn't have to go out into the cold. I sat there meditating. *Why? Why am I going through hell?* Then, like an iceberg, it struck me! You are not allowed to have bad thoughts about someone else. You can't wish that something bad would happen to a person. I'd done just that! On Shabbat afternoon, I was jealous of my son not eating lunch with us—and I wished that his father would miss the plane. Oh my … gosh! What a slap in the face I got from G-d! I vowed *never* to think bad thoughts about anyone again.

With renewed energy, I mobilized the kids, and we went out to the street and headed toward the phone booth. It was occupied. I looked up to the sky and sighed. I noticed that it wasn't snowing. I felt a bit happier, and even though there was snow on the ground, I feel warmer. I spotted a passerby, a religious Jew with long ear lockets, a beard, and a black circular fur hat. I approached him, hoping he would own a cell phone. My cell phone I had left with Pennina. "Can I use your cell phone?" I asked. "I need to call my daughter to call a taxi." With no hesitation, he handed me the phone. "Pennina, please call Union Taxi and try to get Yoni. Gather all our belongings—the stroller and bags—and you and Hadassa and Yaacove meet us in front of the immigration building."

"Okay, Ma," was her stressful reply. We all thanked the religious Jew, and to the fifteenth floor we went.

Sitting and waiting was the hardest thing to do. Time seemed to pass slowly. I read some articles and played the game with six squares and you have to get three X's in a row or three O's but I could not relax until I got the passports in my hands. Natasha's window opened, but there was no Natasha; it was a young black man. My heart stopped, and then he called my name. "Yael Goldmen, can I see your driver's license and your passport, please?" Jotting things down in his documents, he opened my passport and said, "You look happier in this picture." I gave him my winning smile after he returned my stuff and the three brand-new passports. Downstairs, waiting outside the building, I felt we'd won the war against the snow. The sun was shining, and we didn't care that we were cold. We started frantically looking for Union Taxi, which was to arrive at 3:45 p.m. We spotted them, Pennina waving her hand as if it were a victory flag. *London, here we come.*

We checked in at JFK and then waited by the gate. I grabbed my six-month-old, bombarded her with kisses, took the receiving blanket, and started breast-feeding her. I looked up, and there were four friends from the groom's side, friends since nursery school, going to surprise Shimon at his wedding. It was as if the cavalry had arrived as they took control and helped me with the kids' luggage and everything else.

I look at Shimon, now thirty-seven, with three sons and two daughters, and happily he confesses that I was victorious against all odds, that he was so pleased to see me beside him at the wedding. Then he kisses me. My husband, who is beside me on my right, holds my hand under the table and whispers, "I had no doubt you would make it."

Chapter V

Miriam passes me by, tapping my shoulder, and goes to the mike. I think of her fantastic twelfth-grade valedictorian speech—she stole the show. "My emah," she starts, "had another huge mishap. I'm going to let you decide which was worse—almost missing the trip to London ... or the one I'm going to tell you about."

Oh, yes, I remember what she's talking about. It was the summer before the bar mitzvah of Alvin, our first son together. I had planned a fantastic trip with my husband, who would be with us for two weeks, and six children to visit my homeland. From the time we arrived at the airport until thirty days later, all was taken care of. We had VIP service pickup by our tour guide, Choni, and we were staying at the Novetel, only a twenty-minute walk from the Kotel (Wailing Wall). There was an all-you-can-eat breakfast banquet spread, swimming pool, and all the sights we wanted to see. Again, everything was prepaid, even the bulletproof van to the holy sites of our patriarchs, in Chevron. Now you will not believe what happened.

Something looked strange. It was Sunday, 11:28 a.m., and I wondered where the mob of people was. Our whole entourage walked into El Al ticket checking. I took the lead and went around the maze of empty roped-up aisle. A skinny Israeli policeman who was about six feet five gave me a weird look. I faced the agent and handed her eight passports. She was an attractive Israeli woman, her face framed with curly dirty blond hair, half up and half down, and she did not bother to make eye contact. She said confidently, "Your flight leaves at eleven forty this morning."

I came back at her with, "It did not! Our flight does not leave until one forty this afternoon."

"No, ma'am, your flight … I'm checking … Their doors just closed, and they are waiting for permission to take off," she finished.

I pounded my right fist down and demandingly roared, "Well, just open the door right now!" I got someone else's attention, a drop-dead gorgeous man with thick salt-and-pepper hair. Those men are all show but no go! No way! How could I fight this snob who looked like Dean Martin?

"Ma -ha bay ya?" he said, asking me in Hebrew what the problem was.

I'm Israeli too, but I left when I was nine years old, so now I speak broken Hebrew. Therefore, I answered him in English. "We are supposed to be at the Kotel tomorrow. It's my son's bar mitzvah. We bought these tickets more than a year ago. I prepaid for all the hotels and sights. This trip is twenty-eight thousand dollars. My children have nothing to do this summer; we are supposed to be in Israel for over thirty days."

"Send them to camp," was the smart-aleck answer.

"Listen, you, this is not a joke. We don't have the money for camp. We put it toward a family vacation. We are celebrating our son's bar mitzvah, and this is his present! Why didn't anyone call us to let us know you changed the time?"

"Go complain to your ticket agent where you booked the ticket," he said softly, clearly trying to avoid my eyes.

"No way! I will not leave until I get on a plane to Israel," I cried out.

Now I understood why that policeman gave me a weird look earlier: he found it strange that we arrived so late for our flight. He started moving toward me. I stared him down, and my husband intercepted him and informed him that I'm his wife, telling him what just went down. He backed off and said, "Good luck."

The one that looked like Dean Martin came back and said, "I can split you guys up and you can fly on different planes. That's the best I can do."

I looked at his tag and saw that his name was Ehood. "That's nice of you, but I paid much more money for El Al because of the safety. I could have booked a flight with any of the other airlines, but I only trust El Al! Do you get it?"

"Okay, but we don't fly until Tuesday."

"What about our two days of hotel and van and the reservation at the Kotel?"

"You'll have to work that out. Let me see … Do you have a place to stay? And do you need money for a taxi? We can reimburse you."

I just remembered that I'd given up my house for a sheva bracha (a dinner party with the bride and groom after the day they are married) since I was not supposed to be there. Thank G-d it was only the backyard.

We saved our receipts from the taxi, and then we showed up on Tuesday at six in the morning. I was not taking any chances. The children somewhat agreed with me, but they were inconvenienced. At nine o'clock, when the El Al ticket agent opened, we saw a huge five-foot poster stating the following: *Anyone who wants to give up a seat on this flight will receive a free ticket. We over booked seats. Please come see the ticket agent in front.* We had a great laugh as we took a picture beside it.

For all our trouble, Ehood gave us eight free tickets to use anytime within the next year to fly to Israel. At the time, we were excited, but we couldn't spend more money for food and travel during the next year—and where would we stay? So the tickets were a waste, but the trip to Israel was unforgettable!

I'm embarrassed to tell anyone that on the way back, I mixed up day and night, and we missed the return flight. *Here we go again!* They charged us more and got us safely home.

Miriam is now gazing at the crowd with the totals: 55 percent said the London trip was more disastrous; the other 45 percent said the trip to Israel was.

I had to agree. The London trip was more of an emotional drain because I would have missed my son's wedding. On the Israel trip, my husband was accompanying me, and we could always make it up later.

Miriam is book smart. She can write amazing essays, and she makes the best chocolate chip cookies. This year she went to Israel for a year abroad. She came back with twenty-four solid credits that will be transferred to college but more than that; many memories that I will never forget.

She was in the army for eight weeks, and they warned everyone that it was not too late to change their minds, but Miriam insisted. She cried like a baby the first week. She was scolded for not buttoning her top button and forgetting her hat, and she missed breakfast three times when she did not show up with her gun. The first time the troop had to learn to use a gun, Miriam started to whimper. The officer asked her, "What's the matter now?"

She mumbled, "I've never seen a gun before."

When it came to firing the gun, out of all fifty, hers was the only one that jammed. The whole platoon had to wait for Miriam to finish all her bullets—one hour after they had completed theirs. In the army, the officers called her "crybaby." When they passed by each other, they whispered in Hebrew, "Be careful. She cries."

Miriam even cried at the soup kitchen, but that was for a different reason. Her boss told her she was to give out only two meatballs and one scoop of spaghetti. As Miram was following orders, a little girl with black hair in two braids came up to her and spoke in Hebrew, explaining that her little brother could not come and her mom was sick in bed, asking if she could get their food for them. Miriam was overcome with emotion. She carefully placed the two meatballs and spaghetti, then added more meatballs and spaghetti, and repeated that whole procedure again. After that, Miram excused herself from the kitchen and had to take a time out. Miriam had a meltdown; she could not believe how hungry these kids were. She'd grown up in America and had never seen a soup kitchen, even though they did exist. I remember some good times she had working with children in a kibutz, and how she had to be out before the break of dawn to collect the chicken eggs.

Oh, how she has grown. Now she is in college and a whole lot more mature. I feel she does not smile as much as she did before the trip to Israel. She had met this eighteen-year-old boy who spent a lot of time hanging around with her and then went and stupidly promised to marry her. Oh, yeah, I can see that! She realized how dumb it would be long distance, and five years is a long time to wait. Worse, during that wait, he would be allowed to date other people. What a creep! Miriam was smart to break it off, but something happened to her.

I heard on the radio once that character counts. These grandparents had to take care of their grandson who was using vulgar words. The grandpa took the boy to the basement and gave him plywood and nails. He made him hammer a nail for every bad word he used. Then he was to come in and apologize. After hooting and hollering, he did as he was told and came to reconcile with his grandparents. The grandma said, "You go back out now and take each nail out." Confused and upset, the boy marched back and did as he was told. When he came back for the second time, the grandmother broke the silence. "I understand, son. You said sorry, but the holes in the wood are the holes you left in my heart by saying those terrible words to me."

Miriam knows better; I know she got hurt a little. That hole in her heart got filled with Mr. Right. Miram did grate she married a real soldier who is committed and by profession is a pharmacist. She is working on her PA (Physician Assistance) Now she is a mom of a three year old rambunctious boy and an eight month old real doll for a girl. I don't know of any girl who has not had her heart broken one way or another. It is a life experience that all women have to go through.

This year Miriam started her last semester in college. She cried to me on the phone that she had nine finals in one day. She protested that it was impossible. I spoke to her before her hysterics started. I told her that when I prepared a Shabbat dinner for fifty people, I organized myself. One day it was the bread; one day it was the soup and desserts; the next day it was chicken and fish. The dips and salad I do the day of. I can't cook everything in one day! I told her that it's the same with exams; break it up into so many days, timing yourself for each subject. G-d did not create the world in one day. He took six days, and on Shabbat, he rested. When one prepares during the week for Shabbat, he will get to enjoy the day of rest. I told her that when she prepared properly for a test, she would succeed. She started to laugh. She called back and reported that her friends took my advice and were cracking up too.

Now I can see that radiant smile cheek to cheek. She's finished her speech. Miriam lands a kiss on my cheek and hands me an El Al plane gold charm. Speaking of charms, my number two son (he is my lucky charm) gets up to go to the mike. He is quite a performer.

Chapter VI

"I'm going to let you in on how my emah parented us ... and her best-kept secrets," he starts, rolling out a scroll and holding it with two hands. Like toilet paper, his speech keeps rolling down the stage. Seeing this paper come rolling at the audience, everyone laughs uncontrollably. This son, out of all eleven, I think, took me for most of my money and my energy. Now, twenty years later, I see that part of the problem must have been mine. I did not listen to him. Larry was the fourth child and was so tiny that he could not have had anything important to say, or I must have been too busy. But boy, I did learn my lesson.

My best memory with him was teaching him how to read and write. His first book report was about the *Titanic*. He was only in second grade, and I had just gotten married, so we used to go on outings almost every Sunday to get the family to blend together: my original five, David's only child, and two parents. One Sunday we were exploring the *Queen Mary*, and Larry spotted the *Titanic*, its history and pictures posted in glass cases. Because of his keen interest, he got an A plus for the pictures he drew. They were better than the original, and he wrote an amazing one-page report. His teacher, Mrs. Oserof, truly loved my son.

Next we had to read *Island of the Blue Dolphin*. I was pregnant, and toward the end, I left my eight-year-old to read the next three chapters without me. Then, when I came back from the hospital, we would continue reading and brainstorming, completing the report together. After twenty-two hours of labor, my husband and I brought home a beauty. Our first child together, a girl!

Getting back into the routine, I crawled into bed with Larry, and we continued where he'd left off. As we were reading, I found out that there was a new wolf. I thought, when I left off, that the wolf was dead. How did he come back to life? I questioned my honest son. Guess what? He'd never read any of the chapters I asked him to read. Likewise, many times Larry would forget his spelling workbook at school, and after carpool at five o'clock in the afternoon, I would find myself on more than one occasion having to double back and retrieve his books so he could do his homework for the next day. Until he grew up, that boy scared me. I prayed for him more than any child I have raised. At fourteen, he was kicked out of school for hanging around with the wrong crowed. At sixteen, he picked up break dancing, and he is still good at it. However, the rabbis did not approve.

At eighteen, he was enrolled at a yeshiva in New York. We prepaid for the whole year with head checks (posted checks). Within three months, his headmaster had given up on him. I found out the following:

1. Larry informed the teacher he was sick, and after the third day, the rabbi went to see how he was feeling. He found Larry touring Manhattan.
2. Larry came late to class quite frequently. The reason my son gave was that the showers were cold and he had to go to another yeshiva to take a shower.
3. Being in an all boys' school, Larry would socialize with the opposite sex, and during class, he would text message girls.
4. Larry would take limo rides with a gang of boys and girls. He once got so drunk with a girl that he vomited in her parents' house. He had to clean up his mess while intoxicated. Thank G-d Larry had nothing to do with that girl ever again!
5. My cell phone bill was over six hundred dollars in a period of two weeks.

At that point, Larry had nowhere to go, and he was begging to come home. The majority of the people I spoke to said, "You've done all you can. Leave him to straighten up his own mess." How could I do that? Where would he sleep or eat? I couldn't … So my poor husband coughed up the money once more. David flew him back home and supported him until he enrolled in collage.

To appease me, Larry got David and me a real silver Havdala set (candleholder with spice container) that we use to this day. Having Larry at home was a disaster. His room looked as if it had been hit by a tornado, earthquake, and tsunami all at once. For almost six months, he never got up to go to shul and did not bother getting a job. He just hung around like a bum.

My sister-in-law talked some sense into my kid and got him enrolled in a private college, and Larry signed for all his own loans. He registered to get his associate's degree in science, and he was on his way to becoming an architect. While working for a large firm, he got to design cool offices and apartments, including his. Everything was going great, and then Larry was drowning *again*.

Larry got involved with a girl who was straight from the books. She is what you might call an ultra-Orthodox Jew. She would not go into a Gap store if there were inappropriate posters. She would open a holy book after a big Shabbat lunch and lecture us on the lesson. She married a professional man, for my son worked from seven thirty in the morning until seven thirty in the evening daily. Twice a week he went to night school. He got her a brand-new car, and he drove a jalopy around town! She insisted that he go to learn Chacidus (Kabbalah learning) at least twice a week. When was he supposed to rest and unwind? Their marriage lasted three months. But something good did come out of it. I have a smart, great-looking granddaughter named Tzipporah. My son is crazy over her and spends a lot of money on lawyer fees just to so he can see her once or twice a year. She lives on the opposite side of the country.

After the divorce, Larry was so quiet. He was a different person. I on the other hand, broke down. I remember dropping my four-year-old at her class. Her teacher at that time was a twenty-year-old girl named Roxsan. She had gotten close to our family and had seen what we'd all gone through with Larry. She comforted me and said that Larry would find someone new. I burst out crying.

"No one will marry Larry now!"

I hadn't seen it coming. I'd thought everything was roses. I felt hurt because I'd thought I was very close to his ex. We studied together and shared some new recipes for things such as fish chowder soup and salad dressing. Because my son was working day and night, his ex stayed at our house a lot. What happened was for the best, but it did take me for a loop.

That year was my third son's bar mitzvah, so as a present, we took that trip to Israel with the little kids. The whole thirty days, I asked G-d for two things, especially when we prayed at the Wailing Wall. First, I prayed that we would find a suitable nursing home for my mom. That year, she'd come back from Israel poorer than a church mouse. She has Alzheimer's, and we did not know until it was advanced. Second, I prayed that Larry would get remarried.

No joke—when I got off the plane, I got two phone calls. My brother said he was on his way to sign papers, that he was going to admit mom into a nursing home in Vancouver, Canada. Then Larry called to announce, "Get ready to go to Chicago. I'm getting engaged." The girl was Roxsan, my four-year-old daughter's teacher. *At last!* To this day, I love her. Together they gave me a JAP (Jewish American Princess), a granddaughter named Leah.

Larry did pay me back for all the help we gave him—not in money, of course. In 2000, we moved from the big city of Los Angeles to the outskirts of Long Beach. David started working there in the mornings for a philanthropist who needed someone he could trust to take care of his many businesses, and the children started school at the Lubavitch Hebrew Academy in Westminister. We purchased a home of seventeen hundred square feet on a quiet street. In a short time, we had three married children and five grandchildren. When we all got together for barbecues and the holidays, all the married couples occupied the four bedrooms, and the children slept wall to wall on mattresses in the living room. Larry hated my house! He complained that it was over a mile to walk one way to the shul, and the playroom for the children and the place for the adults to hang out were in one area: the living room/dining room. While we were slowly outgrowing our home, I started wishing and praying for a huge house.

We eventually found a place that was over three thousand square feet. One could see the shul from our new home. My husband was not convinced that we could afford the house, or that with our credit, the banks would even look at us. My best friend, Sima, who happened to be a licensed realtor, told my husband that the asking price was $1.5 million, but because it was a short sale, my husband put in a low offer of $720,000. The banks asked my friend if we could purchase it for $770,000. Sima could not believe her ears. She was laughing and trying to explain to the bankers in Texas how special this number was. The rebbe's headquarters in New York is located at 770 Eastern Parkway, and that place had been visited by hundreds of thousands of international people who came to see one person: the Lubavitcher Rebbe, Menachem Mendel. They would ask for advice or for special blessings for their children or businesses. "Of course they will buy the house for that price," Sima assured them.

Larry was in heaven! He took the initiative and drew up plans for a modern state-of-the art kitchen; the rest of the house just needed an upgrade on electrical wiring and the bathrooms as well as a new roof. The cost for those things was $25,000, and now my son was asking for another $100,000 for the kitchen makeover. I had no idea where to get that kind of money. I was set with two toaster ovens and traveling burners that I cooked with in the past when we went on vacations. (Until the day I won the lottery—then I'd have my dream kitchen.) However, Larry did not give up. He kept crunching the numbers, and every time he saw me, he dropped the price of the kitchen by $10,000. When he got to $50,000, that's when, for some reason, I thought I could afford it. It must have been after midnight when I picked up the phone and called my Citibank MasterCard. I explained that I'd bought a new house and would like to remodel, asking if I could max out my credit card. The woman on the phone was so helpful, and she explained that she could either put the money directly into my account or send me a check. Not believing this was real, I asked for the check in the mail, and within five business days, I got $25,000. I tried my Chase Visa, and to my surprise, I got another $25,000. To this day, I can't believe that I got $50,000 just by picking up the phone. I did have a high credit limit, but I never had any use for it. It came in handy that day.

Larry used all his expertise and got the best people he knew on the job. Every day and many nights, he made sure that every nail was put in straight. After all, this was his masterpiece. When all we needed were the knobs for the custom-made mahogany-colored oak cabinets, he told me to choose anything I wanted. I went to Home Depot, and they had ten simple silver knobs for $2.99; I needed sixty-plus knobs. Larry took one look at them and almost puked. I got a call the next morning from my daughter in-law Roxsan. "Emah, you made my husband cry yesterday ..." Not believing what I was hearing, I kept quiet. "Emah, Larry told me that after he put his heart and soul into your extraordinary workplace, where you will be spending a lot of your time, where almost ten people can gather around that island and still not get in your way, you took this poor excuse for a handle and want to throw it on his exquisite workmanship."

I hadn't thought of it like that. I'd never do that. I didn't have the taste to know what went with what. The next day, Larry got six different samples of fancy knobs. All the adults gave their opinions, and when my husband walked in after a late night at work, at around midnight, he and Larry picked the identical ones. To this day, we have those knobs. How much did they cost? Well ... let's just say it was not $2.99. I had to open a Home Depot credit card account.

My son the architect built me a dream kitchen with an island that has a sink; a Passover kitchen, with a kosher milk side with a sink, and a kosher meat side with a sink. There's even a fancy sink in the corner above the wine rack, just for washing hands. The kitchen is really worth $100,000, but because Larry knows a lot about how to build, he did it for half the price. When my husband saw the finished product, he argued with me that he would not let me put department store appliances in. He listened to our son again and got Jenn-Air and KitchenAid. Each had some kind of microscopic scratch that only a trained eye would notice. In case you are wondering which credit card I used for that—I didn't! My loving and hard-working partner used his Bank of America credit card, and with a blink of an eye, he owed $15,000. Now we all look up to Larry and listen to what he has to say. Many of the children use his expertise to fix their surroundings, whether it's inside or outside their homes. He is a genius when it comes to organizing or just making something ugly turn into a place fit for a queen like me. Also, many community members have had their kitchens renovated and hired at that time, this twenty-three-year-old who knows more than many others with all their degrees and experience.

Gazing at Larry on stage, I see a mature, happy man. He had more than paid us back. My prayers had been answered. "Emah," he says, "you had hard times, but you showed us good times. You taught us how to study hard and laugh a lot. When you had to be strict with your left hand, you always cuddled us with the right hand. When we went on outings, we never had much to spend, but you made them fun. You built a strong foundation for us. Emah, you are a tough act to follow. I have three words for you, Emah: *I love you!*" Before I can swallow the lump in my throat, my third son goes up to the mike.

Chapter VII

I SEE THE CROWD ALREADY laughing because of what he's just said: "So basically, first of all ..." I can see that Alvin is nervous. "Uh, yeah ... Okay. Seriously, our emah loves all kinds of games, and she is very mischievous. She starts every water fight ..."

While listening to Alvin, I am remembering the time we were vacationing in Big Bear. We rented a chalet that slept five, plus an adjoining room for the rest of the children. Green Forest Lodge was its name. The grounds were kept up with all kinds of shrubs and flowers; there were rabbits, chickens, and ducks walking around freely. Except that our four younger children, ages six, four, three, and twenty months, did not understand the idea of letting the animals roam around on their own. They wanted to run after them and catch them ... then be nice to them. Alvin, the ninth child of the bunch, caught a fat rabbit, and the rest of the gang followed him into our bedroom, where he plopped the bunny right on top of their father's belly. I don't remember who got the biggest fright, the bunny or my David, who happened to be taking a nap, but the kids succeeded in their great adventure.

This getaway was a pleasure. All the children played, ate, and slept together. The lodge was equipped with a huge swimming pool, basketball court, and tennis court. We also enjoyed the walks around the small town and the hikes up in the hills. In the mornings, because it was vacation, the children loved to sleep in. During the week, they were up at six in the morning to get ready for carpool at seven thirty. David, on the other hand, goes to bed late but can't sleep past six in the morning. He wakes up like an alarm clock and tries to stay in bed until seven thirty, but that's pushing it, so on his own, he got dressed and prayed, and then he got bored or lonely or wanted me to fix him breakfast. At the top of his voice, he would sing, "Good morning to you, good morning to you! We are all in our places with bright shiny faces! Good morning to you, good morning to youuuuuuuu!" That didn't work. So then he'd pull the covers off. We were all annoyed, so we decided to play a trick on him.

We called everyone for a family picture; some sat on the picnic bench in front, and some stood behind or on the sides. I specifically asked David to sit on the back of the picnic bench and save me a seat next to him. I got the manager to come take our photo. I counted one ... two ... In the meantime, the two ten-year-olds, Sophie and Pennina, had gotten a bucket of cold water, and when I said three, we all moved out of the picture, and David got freezing water poured all over him. He yelped so loudly that the neighboring cabin doors opened; the tenants wanted to see what all the commotion was about. We could not stop laughing. All the children made sure to let their father know that this was payback for waking them up during their well-needed restful sleep. The temperature outside was in the nineties, and within thirty minutes, the clothes were all dry, including his *tzizit* (undergarment with four cornerstrings), which he'd screamed about because we did not bring along another pair.

Alvin is our first boy together. When Rivka, our eighth child, was two weeks old, I'd taken her to my father's grave, may he rest in peace. I showed my father my new addition, but then I poured my heart out to G-d, in front of my dad, that David and I should one day also have a son. I had two sons and three daughters from the previous marriage, and David had one daughter six months older than my youngest daughter. When we got married after three years together, I gave birth to two more girls. That made the grand total two boys and six girls.

Growing up with my dad, anything I wanted was always a *maybe*; I never knew where I stood. It would be so easy—yes or no. This time I was surprised. My dad, with the help of G-d, did answer quickly. It was the holiday of Purim, the happiest day in the Jewish calendar, but I was not so happy. I found out that I was expecting. It was crazy! I was already two months along.

I just knew I was going to fall apart. My neighbor of seventeen years invited me for the feast of Purim and secretly whispered to me that she was expecting her sixth child. Thanks to my understanding husband, I had a maid from eight in the morning until two thirty in the afternoon, which is when I had morning sickness, and I would wilt into bed, abandoning my newborn to Elana, a Russian maid. I would forcibly drag myself up and go to carpool, come back, and rush through homework, supper, and baths. I managed to read a story to the whole gang and tuck them into bed. Elana cleaned after supper and folded or did laundry. She left at nine o'clock at night, and I literally felt like dying. How anyone could have two children in one year was beyond my imagination. It was truly a miracle that I survived, and I thank G-d that I had two healthy, gorgeous children in one year!

There's only one downfall. To this day, Rivka complains that we did not take any pictures of her as an infant. She does not get that for the first year of both of the youngest children's lives, their mother was a basket case; it was touch-and-go. I prayed a lot, exercised, and read some darn good books. Both of the children did make it past the teenage years and on to adulthood.

His first four years of life, Alvin had four major operations for his hearing. He had tubes put in. Alvin never spoke clearly, and he was frustrated with his siblings. In school, Mrs. Lapport, his caring teacher, noticed that when she called on Alvin and he was looking at her, he responded, but when he got busy with something and was not looking at her, there was no response. The doctor recommended a fifth surgery; taking my son out of his office, I told the doctor to take a hike! G-d, as usual, sent me an angel. Her name was Nedian Shaw, may she rest in peace. She recommended a chiropractor. Alvin saw Drs. Surnner, a husband and wife team. The chiropractor working there said that as a child, he had had tubes put in his ears twenty-two times. That's when his mother put a stop to that.

Two years after strict orders from the doctor, Alvin was off wheat, flour, sugar, and certain other foods, and his ears improved 100 percent. No more operations. Alvin started to blossom. He loves to read, and he writes expressively; he also enjoys and excels at any kind of sports. He learned to water ski and snow ski in one day. He is great at volleyball, basketball ... you name it. I remember when he was a five-year-old and we used to go to the park. After the kids got bored with the equipment, we always played tag. The kids would yell, "That's not fair, Daddy! You only chase Emah!" The kids did not have to worry. Within ten seconds, I would be caught if I didn't have any obstacles around me to hide behind. But no matter how much David tried, he could not catch Alvin. He was our little gingerbread man on the loose. In school, Alvin's name went permanently on a wall, stating that he did over 101 step-ups in one day when competing against kids his age. Today, Alvin towers over his father by three inches, and my David is no shorty!

Alvin finishes explaining how when we played a card game or board games, three-fourths into the game they would find me, Emah, cheating. Alvin has the whole audience in his pocket. He concludes with, "Emah, you made me who I am today. Emah, you rock! Thank you!"

Just as he is returning to his seat, Rivka intersects him and whispers, "Wish me luck."

Chapter VIII

THIS GIRL GLOATING IN FRONT of the microphone is an exception. In all her twenty-three years, 99.99 percent of the people she encounter love her. My eighth pregnancy, Rivka's, was a scary one. Because I was over thirty-five, they made me feel as if I didn't belong at the doctor's office. I'd had my chance at having babies. I'd had enough … and how dare I have more. The exam revealed that the brain was developing much faster than the other parts of the body, and she would be deformed. After two referrals, the doctors all agreed that I should abort! Not knowing what to do, we faxed a letter to our rebbe at Seven-Seventy, and sure enough, the answer came back three different times—to leave well alone.

As if to bribe us, Kaiser wanted to pay for us to go see a top specialist at Cedar Sinai Hospital. I recall that day of judgment, what my husband shared with me. We were getting ready for the appointment, and we had time to kill, so we walked around the dingy block. My husband passionately started speaking. I came to a halt and looked into his eyes. They were glossy and moist. Forcefully, he moved his quivering lips. "Listen, I know you've been though a lot, but no matter what, I love you and this baby. I don't care what it looks like. I will love it!" That did it for me; we never kept that appointment. We called Rivka our new addition, and standing before us now is a gorgeous girl, as beautiful and precious on the inside as she is on the outside.

Before I delight you with her amazement let me tell you I could not have made it with two babies if it were not for our Rivka. (Overall she was an easy baby, if I would have had Alvin first I don't think I would have been able to handle two babies eleven months apart.) The first three months, she had her days and nights mixed up, but because the baby I was expecting was due in a few months, I had some time to help her learn the difference. When Alvin, our ninth child, was born *the same year*, Rivka thought it was her very own doll. She automatically zoomed her index finger toward Alvin's eyes. She made nice three times, and after the fourth, she slugged him in the face and then said how sorry she was, trying to give him a kiss.

She grew up faster than most babies did. The first day of school, her father escorted her. He came home and reported about her first fifteen minutes of encountering her classmates. The teacher had a bowl of colorful crayons and paper on the table so the children could sit down and get busy. Rivka assertively pulled a boy's hand out of the bowl and explained that you could only take one color at a time. The boy was sitting across from her. She proceeded to give each child at her table one crayon. During circle time, she told on a little boy who had his thumb in his mouth—while she kept her fingers dry. The teacher gave strict instructions to everyone that there was no sucking of any fingers, and that they should be dry at all times. Rivka sucked two fingers from her right hand, her index and the thumb; many times teachers and family members had to remind her that she was a young lady and she had to keep her fingers dry too. We had to put in an instrument in her mouth for a year to prevent an overbite. It worked, except that she started talking much more and never stopped. My husband picked her up from a sleepover at her cousin's house once, and the whole forty-five-minute ride, she kept jabbering on and on.

Motor mouth and all, she is such a kind person. Even at the young age of four, when my nephew David Shallom cried because he was the only one not to get a Mickey Mouse lollipop, as I explained earlier, she took her last lick and asked us to wash off her germs once she parted with her candy. (Incidentally, at his bar mitzvah, David Shallom gave

Rivka a huge lollipop, repaying his debt. He never forgot the little girl's sacrifice, and neither could we.)

Fast-forwarding to elementary school, Rivka was still a character. On her way to school, she didn't get her way once, and as my husband was strolling along with the other kids to class, our little Rivka was crying. Her teacher happened to see her, and she said, "Oh, Rivka, your tears don't usually start till the afternoon, during math." Rivka loved the underdogs in her class. She befriended a Persian girl, and for a whole year, she entertained us by imitating her friend's accent and talking about how she got along in school. Today they are inseparable.

Rivka loves to read, and during those years at school, there would be a monthly competition for who read the most books. Rivka won most of the time, but once, David Polter, her opponent, whom she disliked, had the same amount of points. Both students were called to the principal's office. As they were walking, one asked the other, "Did you tattletale on me?" Obviously, no one was accusing them of anything. They were simply going to be awarded at the monthly ceremony for the highest achievement for Reading Counts. This incident was written up in the school newspaper—for when the principal asked them if they knew why they were there, she found out that they both thought that they had ratted on each other.

One not-so-nice memory was of a bully that had lashed out at my daughter. As I was brushing her curly wet hair, she cringed and jumped. I was very gentle; I had saturated her hair with conditioner, so there was no reason for her to be in such pain. I finally dragged the story out of her. That day, a gorilla of a classmate, who was two times my daughter's height and age (he'd had to repeat a grade), was verbally abusive with the teacher and then turned to the child next to him, who happened to be Rivka, and he screamed profanity, violently plopping a math book on my daughter's head. As if that weren't enough outrage, he grabbed a science book and threw it at a moving target, my daughter's back. The colorful rainbow of a line down my daughter's spine got my blood boiling. I demanded from the headmaster of the school that the perpetrator be suspended from school for a couple of days. I wanted some kind of retribution. I did not get it!

The next day, I called the police and met an officer at the school at nine o'clock the next morning. What a waste of my time. After a whole hour of talk between the principal (who looked as if he should have retired four years earlier), the police officer, and me, the kid got only a report on his record, not even a reprimand. I took matters into my own hands and talked to the parents. I got a surprising answer: "Yes, he does that at home too." Not satisfied, I put my face only two inches away from the gorilla's face and threatened that if he even thought of touching anyone in my family again, I would make mincemeat out of him. Then I yelled at the top of my voice, "Do you understand!" Incidents with this gorilla and other kids have happened, but nothing has been done. I'm just waiting until he is an adult and commits a serious crime; then it will be all over the news how this guy had a record of violence and abuse, but no one had the guts to take care of him properly. Anyway, that boy graduated and got out of my children's school, so they were safe for a while, until they meet with him on the street.

My grown-up Rivka helps everyone in the family, and when anyone needs a babysitter, she is the first to take the job, even if it means staying up late at night and then coming home and continuing to do her homework. She has a job teaching Sunday school every week, and at our temple on Saturday mornings, during Shabbat services, while the adults pray, she takes care of forty kids under six years of age. The list goes on ...

I see she has started her speech. "Our emah has her very own vocabulary. She says she wants to go to 'Barneble Knowbels' instead of Barnes and Noble; 'Spacebook' instead of Facebook; and 'Gilgul'— in Hebrew, it means reincarnation—instead of Google. She calls our English teacher, Mr. Franks, 'Rabbi Frankel.' Thirty years ago, my oldest brother's first-grade teacher was a Rabbi Frankel. My emah can't remember anyone's name, so as not to embarrass others or herself, she greets all she meets with, 'Hello, gorgeous.' Me, well, I have ten siblings so I have ten other names besides my given name. Emah gets so busy that she points to me, and each time her voice gets louder: 'Miriam … I mean, Pennina … Alvin … No … Hadassa … Please come …' She takes a breath and then finally calls my name, but by then, she's forgotten what she wanted. She says 'camp cam' instead of webcam; she can't say any words that have the letter *r* in them; and she says 'UFB' instead of USB.

"Now I'm going to ask you a question," my daughter continued. "Would you buy a brand-new car for yourself and the family to use if you don't know how to drive the car?" I glance at the audience; no hands have gone up. "Well, that's what my mother did when she bought a new computer. In the seventeen years that I have lived with her, she has bought at least five computers, and to this day, she does not know how to use them. It's like owning a car and someone always calling you, asking how you start it. It would be okay … but not after a million times. I could be doing my homework, or be on my computer, or best yet, in bed with a good book, and I would hear, 'How do I put a comment on Spacebook?' or 'How do I download my pictures without deleting the ones in my camera?' or "How do I send an e-mail with a picture?" or 'I want personalized stamps; how do I print them?' It goes on and on.

"She once took my laptop to New York, and she successfully put in a disk to show off the slide show to family, but then she didn't close the laptop properly so it did not turn on. The screen was black no matter which button she pushed. She was afraid to tell me. A week passed. I joined her in New York with my friend, and she secretly confided to my friend that she broke my laptop. My friend Analis advised her to take out the battery and start the program again. My emah did as instructed and voilà … it worked! Emah did the same thing with an iPod. She bought three of the children for good behavior their very own iPods. When it came time for her to use it during her walk or on the treadmill, it was disastrous. She did not know how to turn it on or how to choose songs—and forget downloading any tunes. She always called on one of the teens at home. Even our little Hadassa, who was seven, knew how to work and even charge her very own iPod. My present to you is six private lessons on how to use your own computer and iPod, but Emah, if it's okay with you, I will *not* be your teacher. I love you tons, Emah. I can't live without you. You add a lot of laughter to my life."

We kiss and hug tightly. As she returns to her two twin boys and husband (Yizchack) I remember kissing him tightly too. Years ago at the doctor's office while we were waiting, he was interacting with my Rivka. I fell in love with him then and gave him a kiss and a bear hug. (Yizchack was four) Speaking of laughter, I have a son who, at thirteen, always used to get in trouble for laughing. Can you imagine? Here he goes now. He's five feet six inches tall and looks just like my dad did when he was nineteen. Yaccove is handsome and slim, with dark curly hair, and he is known to his siblings as "the little man."

Chapter IX

"Hello, everyone. I'm the last boy, the tenth addition in the family, so obviously the best." As he starts speaking, I remember that time when he was punished for disturbing the class because he cracked up aloud, but then, so would I. Let me explain. Rabbi Lampport was preaching that the Chapter Tezave, from 613 commandants, has the highest percentage of commandments … It has 9 percent. Who would not emit a small chuckle when expecting to hear 88 percent or 99 percent, but 9 percent—that's a joke. So "the little man" got a strict talking-to, and he promised to act more respectably in class.

In second grade, Yaacove started reading Harry Potter books. I was impressed. One summer night I will not forget, I put Yaacove and his brother to bed with a story and kisses. Then I continued to the girls' room and did the same. As I was about to retire for the night, Yaacove asked for me. I was exhausted and could not wait to fall into bed with a good book. "Yes, my Yaacove, what is it?"

"I hear a hissing sound from under my bed," he innocently complained.

I brushed it off. "Just go to sleep; it's the books you've been reading." I left the door ajar, and then my Rivka, eight at the time, called on me too.

"Emah, I heard a thump in my room." I turned on the light and saw nothing. Again ready to dive into my own bed, I assured her that nothing was wrong and told her to go to sleep.

The next day, we were getting ready to celebrate our last child's first birthday. The whole family would join us for pizza and a cake made in the shape of a Barbie doll. The two eight-foot tables were set with the pink tea set theme, and balloons were touching the ceiling above, their pink-and-white strings hanging down. I had the maid cleaning the bathrooms and bedrooms, so I went to check by the desk in the boys' room. Between two twin beds rested an oak student desk. But behind the desk, you could find a lot of dust if the housekeeper did not remove it once a week. So I had time on my hands and decided to take matters in my own hands and move the desk. "Aaaaah!" I screamed. I jumped on the bed next to the window and then leaped off and dashed out the bedroom door, banging it shut behind me. What had I seen? My brain could not register this animal. It was not a mouse, and it was not a rat. My heart was pounding, and I was shaking.

Rueven, my son in-law, happened to drop by to pick up my electric drill. "What's the matter?" he questioned, looking at me, petrified.

"The ... the ... the ... there's a strange animal in there," I mumbled.

He proudly stated, "Don't look at me. I can't even kill a spider. Channah gets them—lizards, cockroaches, frogs—and she discards them in the trash." Channah is their one-year-old daughter and my first granddaughter.

Great! What should I do? I kept holding the door shut tight; I did not want the creature coming out. The handyman who was painting my white picket fence walked into the house, and I explained to him that as I went to move the desk, I saw something that looked like a huge rat but wasn't. It had a stiff tail, long nose, furry body, and black boulders for eyes. It popped out and nonchalantly tiptoed from behind the desk, going under the twin bed by the wall. That's Yaacove's bed. I felt so guilty for not believing my little man. The handyman, being more courageous than my son-in-law and me, entered the room. Not one to take any chances, I closed the door behind him.

Two seconds later, he came out and announced, "It's a possum. They come out at night. They're blind as a bat during the day. But boy, do they have sharp teeth. Come see; he's in the corner."

Walking close behind this seventy-five-year-old skinny English man, I bent down, and there he was—like a fat rabbit but not cute at all ...and those eyes! One look was all I needed, and I dashed out. I was suspecting that the men putting down our new wood floors must have left the door open—and that's how the creature let himself in. Among the three of us, we came up with a solution. I picked up the phone to call my husband. Luckily, he was working in town so he would be on time for his little girl's first birthday celebration. When David heard about the catastrophe, he started to laugh uncontrollably, and then he soundly advised me to call the police as he continued cracking up. I picked up the phone and called 911.

"This is the police department. Is this an emergency?"

"Yes! There is a possum in my house, under my son's bed. I have five kids under the age of nine, and it's my one-year-old's birthday party in a few hours."

I was rudely interrupted. "Sorry, that is not police business; call animal control," and all I could hear was a dial tone. Slamming the phone down, I broke down, thinking what that monster would have done to my children. I felt so guilty for ignoring my Yaacove's fears last night.

I got animal control on the phone. I explained my situation, and she had the nerve to come back with, "Is the animal dead? Is the animal a cat or a dog?" She refused to help.

Unable to control my temper, I assertively and loudly tried to explain: "I'm alone in the house," I lied, "except for my one-year-old, whose birthday party is today. We're going to have a lot of children here, and someone is going to get hurt. How would you like it if, G-d forbid, one of my children gets bitten and ends up in the hospital? I will tell them that I spoke to a certain Sheila from animal control, and she refused to help because the creature is not a dead cat or a dog!"

"Sorry, ma'am," was her response, and the line went dead. Looking at Rueven and my handyman, I could not speak.

Not even ten seconds passed, and the doorbell rang. Opening the door, I saw a man towering there. He had a khaki uniform on and a sewn-on badge showing him as a legal animal trapper. This six-feet-nine, husky white male had to bend his head to come into my house. As he put on his heavy-duty gloves, he got the information as to where exactly the possum was hiding. We soon heard the beds scratching the floor and the pounding of footsteps. With a calm voice, he said, "I got him."

I opened the door to the room, and there was a fat possum in the man's hands. "Please wait. I want to get my camera. Otherwise, no one will believe me." As I snapped the picture, the possum took off and dove under the bed. I slammed the door. For the second time, the man caught the possum, and he marched outside with him and let him go past my gate. Many years later, I apologized to Yaacove in front of 168 people at his bar mitzvah for not responding to his dangerous situation.

There was another situation but not quite so scary. As Yaacove grew up, he loved to read books. In fifth grade, he got an award for Reading Counts, and each month, the principal would call on Yaacove for having read the most books that month and taking a comprehensive test on each. He has ten medals. Once, a rich uncle of a girl in Yaacove's class threatened to switch the Reading Counts to his niece so she could win. I was naive and was super worried. Yaacove assured me that it couldn't be done. When Yaacove approached sixth grade, he did not want to be on Reading Counts; he would read on his own. He wanted the girl in his class (Rachel was her name) to win; she too loved books. I agreed.

My Yaacove is very competitive and is successful in any sport. He shares his love for cars with me. As we drive together, he points out the Corvettes, Porsches, and Lamborghinis. I can spot an Audi and a BMW, but I get mixed up with Cadillacs and Continentals. One time at a dinner party, he ran to the parking lot and saw a Maserati. He took a picture with his iPod. My son's dream is to own a Mustang or a Corvette and have a personal license plate reading DRMCAR. I remember six years ago, he asked when I would have time to take him driving. He is only thirteen. No way!

My first son drives with one hand on the steering wheel and does not listen when I ask him to stop directing his right hand every place but the wheel. My second one to drive, Devorah had to repeat the driving course twice; no matter how hard she tried, she could not stay in her lane. Shoshana drove so close to the parked cars that my husband once screamed so hard that she began to cry and never drove with him again. She once persuaded me to let my eighteen-month-old boy go with her on a small errand. She showed up two hours later, her face all puffed up and red, and I could not console her or reprimand her. Shoshana ran to her room and locked the door behind her. I found my key and, against her wishes, opened the door. I found her doubled over and murmuring in silence. "What in the world has gotten into you? What happened?" I questioned. My mind was rolling one hundred miles per hour. What could have happened? Did someone touch her? Did someone hurt her? I could not understand what all the drama was about. Unable to stand it anymore, I blurted out, "I'll kill him … Who is it?"

She took a deep breath, then looked at me and said, "No one!" I held her, and she cried her eyes out for another five minutes. Then she started to explain. "I was in an accident."

"Oh, my baby, is that all?"

"Emah, I totaled a Porsche." I hugged her, and she continued. "I turned around for Yaacove, and the seven-passenger Dodge Ram not only hit an actress's car but went on top and smashed it." That accident cost us three thousand dollars. Thank G-d no one was hurt.

Larry learned to drive next; he backed out from the parking lot and, sure enough, scratched a rabbi's car. That only cost us five hundred dollars. Larry does not listen to my barking either. He once asked me to come with him to a car rental business. That Friday morning, as he was driving, I warned him to go slow in an intersection with only two stop signs. A car coming from the left of us was going at top speed and ran right into us. It hit the passenger door on the driver's side. Luckily, Larry had control of the car, and he tried to calm me down. "Oh G-d!"

I yelled repeatedly, and Larry just kept the car spinning. It was going at top speed until he got it to slow down. If I would have been driving, I would have been killed. There was a huge Dumpster on the right-hand side, and if I were trying to stop the car without slowing it down, we would have flipped or crashed head-on into the Dumpster. Yes, I have to admit that Larry drives very fast, but that day, he saved my life.

Pennina was next. I did not even bother. By the time she was ready, I had another baby at the house, and there was no way I could be driving anywhere with the lack of sleep I was getting. She learned to drive on her own. She is braver than I am. For a year, she drove daily from New Jersey to New York. I can trust her to drive because she is so cautious.

Sophie learned with her mom, and she was not bad. At one intersection, as Sophie was trying to drive through, a man drove her right into a light post. She had to go to a few months of physical therapy, and she ended up with a settlement.

Miriam still has no concept of what driving is all about. Back in the day, she would not notice pedestrians in the crosswalk. I would have to scream at her to stop. She went through a red light once. Thank G-d nothing happened … but still. She passed the test after her second try. That was a true miracle. She has not driven a car since. G-d better help the people around Miriam when she gets behind the wheel!

Rivka, our next driver, was promised by her dad that he would take her to school once a week and let her drive. I take her driving early in the morning or late at night, when the streets are not so busy.

One time when my husband was in the car, ready to take Rivka out, I was on my way back from dropping the children off at the bus stop. I saw her flagging me down as she pulled up next to me. I rolled down my window and saw that Rivka was not happy. "Emah, can you please drive with me? I don't want to drive with Daddy."

"Why?" I grunted.

"Daddy stopped breathing as I drove out of the driveway, and when I questioned him about what was wrong, he just yelled and threw his hands up in the air."

I looked at David, and he did have a guilty look as he got out and we switched cars. I exchanged words with him. "There go my plans for the day."

"Thank you for your patience," he responded.

I just didn't have a choice. I sat there holding on to the door handle and the seat, my legs glued to the floor. My face was tense, and I did not talk unless it was totally necessary. If my mouth was opened, it was going to start throwing out commands: you're going too fast; you hit the curb; you're too close to the boat; use more gas when you're going uphill; stop; check over your shoulder … When they were first learning how to control the car, I used to take them to a cemetery. I didn't have to worry about them killing anyone because the people there were already dead. Teaching children how to drive is one chore I despise!

I felt bad for Rivka that day. She paid for her own driving school lessons; she insisted that it was not a necessity, and that we did not have to shell out our hard-earned money. I pray that whomever she marries will not only be as smart and attractive as she is but have a kinder heart than hers, if that is possible.

My friend Sima takes Rivka driving at six in the morning. (Rivka, from all the kids, is the only one who agreed to that early time, and after her morning prayers, she has her permit with her and is ready to go. Sima loves it that no one is on the road so Rivka can drive as slowly as she wants. I have three more to get through driving school. Maybe by then, I will win a lottery and let the school teach them until they pass the test … and then some.

As my son is finishing his speech, I hear him say, "Emah, thank you for raising me with strictness and a touch of humor." I hear cheering and clapping for my tenth child. He is a bit of a wisea—, if you ask me.

Chapter X

Now I CAN SEE MY redheaded daughter come up to the stage. She too is witty and smart, the only daughter with whom I had no birth pains. Sophie is my husband's only daughter from a previous marriage. She joined our blended family when she was four years old.

We all laid our eyes on her for the first time when she was about three and a half. David and I had started to date, but before we could move to the next level in our relationship, we wanted the children to meet. That day, David was on time; he drove a silver Chrysler, and he pulled up across the street. The door opened, and David walked around, got this gorgeous, shaggy redheaded, sleepy doll out of the car and set her on the trunk. She wore a sleeveless summery dress with a ruffled hem. He proceeded to put on her shoes. Finally, he carried his daughter to our front door. The children all got along with her from the first moment they saw her.

We all sat down for dinner; pepper steak and fried rice became the family's favorite. Everyone chatted and answered questions when asked, except for Sophie. We excused the children to the playroom, and David and I cleared the table. (Now, twenty years later, I have to nudge him more than once to give me a helping hand, and begrudgingly he does.) Not five seconds passed, and Shimon, the oldest, followed by the rest of the children, ran down the hall screaming, "She talks, she talks, she talks." It was a memorable night.

After we got married, Sophie came to us every Thursday, which used to be library night. Sophie had started to read early, and she introduced our family to many great books like the Nancy Drew series as well as classics like *Pollyanna* and *Black Beauty*. I was excited and many times got emotional about reading these books. The part in which Pollyanna has to sleep in the attic while her spinster aunt has an old mansion with five other bedrooms unused ... Yes, the kids saw me crying. You see, coming from Israel at nine and half years, I spoke broken Old English. The first book I actually enjoyed and finished was in the seventh grade, so all this new literature was a real treasure, and I was like a kid in a candy store. Reading was relaxing and a great way to spend the last part of the day with the kids.

However, I was skeptical about the *Goosebumps* series. I looked at a cover of one of the books and wanted to scream. My husband assured me that they would enjoy the book. I stood my ground and growled back, "No way." The book was a paperback, and the title was *Welcome to Camp Nightmare*. The book is about two hundred pages, and I would have finished it in one night, but because of all the interruptions, and because I had to have some sleep, I finished it in three days (after my chores, of course), staying up past midnight. I *loved* the book; it was so cleverly written. I could not stop some nights because I was so scared that I had to read on to see what would happen. Now my grandsons are reading it.

Sophie also came on weekends. Saturday nights after Shabbat, we allowed the kids to watch a Disney movie. When it was time for bed, Sophie was asked to pick up her pillow, and I remember her comment as if it were yesterday. At the age of four and a half, she dragged her pillow behind her and said, "She makes me work and work." Sophie, being the only child, was pampered a little more than the other kids were by her biological mother. Her chores at her mother's home were to wake up with a smile, open up the shades, exercise, feed the cat and dog, and get all her homework done. As for cleaning her room, well, her mother tried to get her to do it.

Once when David was taking Sophie home, she had him sign her report card with bad grades. David did, but he was sworn to secrecy by his daughter never to tell her mother. Feeling a bit guilty, my husband called Dr. Laura for advice. Dr. Laura's answers are always straight. She said to show some backbone and tell her mother. David answered, "I will, and I'll tell my daughter you said so."

In our house when the children were growing up, no one got a bandage unless there was blood. That rule changed because Sophie sometimes arrived with many colorful bandages of different characters decorating her legs from the knee down. Having Sophie six months younger than Pennina, my youngest baby at the time, there was a tad bit of jealousy. At age four, Pennina came up to me and asked that I not get angry if she asked me a question. I stopped what I was doing and got down on my knees so I could be at her eye level. I knew something was up. She was nervous and looked all around except for in my eyes. She kept saying, "I won't be sad, I promise. I just want to know the truth." I stopped her hands from gesturing all over the place and then cupped her chipmunk cheeks, promising I would not lose my temper.

"Emah …" She hesitated. "Do you love me or Sophie more? I won't be sad—just tell me who you love more."

My knees could not hold me up, and as they buckled, I plopped to the floor. "Oh, my funny Pennina, you are my baby."

"I know," she insisted "but, Emah, who do you love more? I want to know. Who do you love more?"

I got off the floor, not letting go of my chubby four-year-old, and held her close to my chest. "Of course I love you, but I love Sophie too, just like I love Shimon, Devorah, Shohanna, and Larry. *All the same!*" She did not buy it. I tried again, this time using visual senses. I set up two unlit candles. "Pennina, when I light a candle and take its flame to light another, it does not make the fire smaller than the first one."

Pennina did not believe me at the time, but many years later, when she was twenty-three and a mother to a three-month-old, I reminded her of her personal dilemma. She did remember, and we laughed, of course. She then asked the same question all over again. "But how can I love the next baby if I love this baby so much?" I reassured her that she had enough love to go around—for her husband and many more children.

This problem of clinginess was never part of Sophie's character. The first time we went on vacation, Sophie's mother was so concerned that we were going for a week, and that Sophie had never left her side for that long. Her mother had no choice but to compromise and send Sophie with an album. The nine-by-fourteen book consisted of pictures of Sophie with her mom and pictures of the dog and cat. Worried that we would lose the precious photos, I volunteered to carry them in my handbag. Sophie did not ask for them. Not once! Not even after she spoke to her mother every night to say good night, which was like a chore for her because she would have to stop what she was doing and either make a phone call or receive one. Sophie would rather have a grand time with so many playmates. It was like a slumber party every night.

In our stopover at Monterey Bay, we stayed at a grand hotel, with two queen-size beds in each room. The two boys and four girls took turns, each sleeping one night on the beds and one night on the floor. It was the little girls' turn to sleep on the bed, and my oldest son, Shimon, who was ten at the time, was irritating Sophie and Pennina, trying to convince them that they should sleep on the floor because they were the youngest. David walked in, and they continued to battle it out. I walked in and give Shimon a stern warning look, explaining that this was Sophie's first family vacation, and before I could finish my sentence Sophie commented, "Yeah, Shimon, I've wished for a family all my life." We all chuckled, but she was right. Having all this love made her even more secure.

When she grew up, she attended NYU and graduated with a bachelor's degree in theater. She later got her license to teach yoga. Sophie comes to all our family gatherings, and she even put on everyone's makeup for Larry's wedding. She is still close to Pennina, and she still calls me Emah.

One day when she was about six, she surprised me when she came up to me while I was washing dishes. In her hand was a present wrapped in khaki-colored paper, with a ribbon running around all the corners, making a six-leaf ribbon. I remember admiring the silk lilac material as I unraveled it. When I opened the package, there in the center was a gray-pink clay masterpiece with painted seashells, which she had made for me for Mother's Day. To this day, I have her gift on my bay window, and it reminds me of her kindness.

Another time, I awakened cranky because the night was hard with one of the babies. Sophie suggested I eat breakfast, telling me that it would calm me down. She had prepared eggs and toast just for me.

Today, seeing her stand in front of everyone is so pleasurable. She finishes her speech by thanking me for making her dream come true and giving her what she could never have: four brothers, six sisters, thirteen nieces and nephews, and lots and lots of love. "Thanks, Emah." Sophie and I kiss and hug. I give her a blessing in her ear that one day soon she too will have fun raising her own children. I was blown away when she informed me secretly that she was seeing an amazing guy, an Israeli like me. He is in cooking school and loves children. I hug her tight with delight, and as we untangle, I want to hear more about this Mr. Right, but I see Pennina giving Sophie a high five as she approaches the front.

Chapter XI

Pennina, now a new mother herself, is at the mike with her killer smile. She stands five feet tall, and her husband towers over her by a foot. At our home, when Pennina was a lot younger, I would give many treats for good behavior or sometimes for special occasions. At times, Sophie would not be present, because it was not on her scheduled day to visit, so I would save her treats for when we would see her again. Once we all got special decorated cupcakes, and I left one in the fridge for her. The next day, I pulled out the plate to give Sophie her special cupcake and saw that the icing from one side had been licked off. I assembled each one of my children at that time—the oldest was nine and the youngest, Pennina, was three—and I started to interrogate, but no one wanted to admit guilt. "Shimon, did you touch Sophie's cupcake? Devorah, Shoshana, Larry, tell the truth. I won't get angry. Pennina?"

I saw Pennina twist from side to side and then go up on her tiptoes. Then, with her baby voice, she blurted, "Let's not talk about it."

Buying clothes was difficult at times because only some kids would get new clothes, while others got hand-me-downs. Many times, Pennina often got Sophie's clothes. We were at T.J. Maxx, and I recall Pennina having a temper tantrum because she wanted a new bathing suit like Sophie's. I would have done it, but I'd just spent three hundred dollars on summer clothes for all six kids, and if I could save twenty dollars, why throw away money? Pennina could not understand that she had her old suit and Sophie's top-of-the-line Speedo bathing suit from the previous year, which was hardly worn.

Another time, at Sophie's kindergarten graduation, Sophie dressed up in her special dressy outfit. Pennina had the same outfit, and she insisted on wearing it the same day. I tried several times to explain that it was not her party and she didn't need to wear a dressy outfit. The whole day she was cranky, and in a bad mood and teary-eyed, she followed me with her pudgy little arms folded across her chest.

Pennina, like Sophie, had to be shared by her dad; she would go there every other weekend. One time the kids came home and relayed how Pennina excitedly explained to everyone present that she had two dads. She had Daddy in Emah's house and Abah, which means father in Hebrew, at Grandma and Grandpa's house. Her biological father got so angry that he practically turned red trying to explain to a three-year-old that she only had one father. Pennina's father did show his disappointment in me for allowing the kids to call their stepfather Daddy. I pointed out to him that according to the Torah, the children cannot call an adult by his or her first name.

When she wants something, Pennina can be as stubborn as an ox. When she was finally growing up and her teenage years were almost over, she got a job, like her sister the previous year, as the head counselor of Long Beach Gan Israel. She had the responsibility of over a thousand children who attended the camp. She had to make sure the instructors were with their classmates at all times. Three things were stressful for her: the kinds of food her sixty teachers would be served daily, trip days, and writing the end-of-the-week journals to send home to the parents.

In the mornings, it was a no-brainer: some grabbed a bowl of Raisin Bran cereal, some grabbed a yogurt with a granola bar, and the few that were usually asleep on the job rolled out of bed five minutes before the van was ready to take off, coming to camp starving, only to indulge in high-calorie doughnuts of different kinds. (A study was done on April 20, 2010, revealing that Kellogg's Raisin Bran cereal has about twenty grams of sugar, while Rise Krispies only has three grams of sugar. So much for eating healthy; they might as well have joined their friends and had doughnuts.)

Lunch was no biggie either. It was served at school if you preordered, so the counselors got their lunches as an added bonus. Same routine day in and day out: Monday was chicken; Tuesday was spaghetti and meat sauce; Wednesday was pizza; Thursday was tacos; and Friday was hot dogs.

But when it came to supper, that was hard. Many times the girls were starving; either they missed supper because they overworked at the school, or there was not enough food. Whatever the reason, Pennina, like Shoshana before, used to come to my house, grab pots, and help herself to my freezer to cook dinner for the forgotten group. I would likewise be talked into having the counselors for Friday night dinner. That was great because they used to hang around and sing until all hours of the night.

The trips were so difficult to plan; sometimes the boys' camp also came to the same amusement park. But the rule was they could not be seen together or even talk to each other. That is great, but how do you explain that about 60 percent of the boys' head counselors ended up marrying the girls' head counselors? I had no such luck with my daughters. Occasionally, the buses came late to school because a kid was missing or the counselor misjudged the time, and everyone had to wait for the last group to come strolling back with no guilt or remorse.

The best part of Pennina being a head counselor was her letters she had to send to parents. David told me the story. Pennina would call between four and five in the evening and ask David for help on writing something clever. David was happy to oblige and would take time to rhyme the message, sometimes adding cheerful jokes. David stressed how initially she would thank him profusely. "Oh, Daddy, you're the best. This is so great—thank you, thank you." Then she repeated this chore a few more times and made sure David complied, but the thank-yous became shorter and fewer. She once forgot about a letter, and though it was half past midnight, she picked up the phone and called David at work. She was lucky he was still there; he was just turning off the lights to come home. "Oh, Daddy," she said sweetly, "I have to have this letter by Friday. Can you help?" David explained that he was retiring for the night, but Pennina would not take no for an answer. "Oh, Daddy, come on. You can do it. Just do it!"

Pennina was quite a catch. She went out with this twenty-five-year old who made it in real estate with his father's money. Now he rents and manages the properties. He dated my daughter for three months, taking her to steak houses in New York and spoiling her by buying trinkets. Then one afternoon he called her at work and said that he was breaking up with her. By the time she called me, she had excused herself from the rest of the day's work and was driving in a blizzard. She was crying hysterically. We had all believed this would be the one. I made her pull into a gas station and stop driving. She stopped the car but could not stop crying. I offered to fly there for a few days. Hearing how worried I was, she calmed down a little and started from the top, explaining every disgusting detail of the breakup. A week later, this air head sent my Pennina an expensive iPod that could do everything but cook. I did not have to tell her what to do with it. With pleasure, she sent it back: RETURN TO SENDER; ADDRESS UNKNOWN. The jerk tried to keep in touch, but Pennina asked the playboy never to call again.

Thank G-d that after dating twenty-two duds and going to school to get her license as a personal trainer, she found the man of her dreams. They got married on this very ship, the *Queen Mary*, in 2009. That wedding cost me forty grand, and I'm still paying it off. It will take me at least four more years to pay it off.

We had such a mix-up with the number of guests coming from out of town. Invited guests usually would not have flown, but because they heard it was on the *Queen Mary*, they looked forward to the adventure. Her friends alone were thirty teenagers flown in from Israel, England, New York, and as far away as Australia, and they did not stop dancing for a second. The groom I did not know; he had such a huge family that 120 came, and they were all cousins, uncles, and aunts that lived right here in Los Angeles. I'd pictured a wedding for 150 guests. I got 330 responses, and 279 showed up. She did get her dream wedding.

Her chuppah (a wedding canopy) overlooked the Pacific Ocean. It was a clear day—not a single cloud, no wind, no outside noise—just your perfect summer day in March.

At this moment, Pennina finishes her speech by thanking Daddy and me for giving her a security blanket full of love and kindness and warmth. She promises that she will instill that in her own family, and with that, she passes by me and gives me a hug. She then continues to her seat next to her husband, who is holding their infant, baby Moshe. Pennina is my fourth girl, and now I am going to introduce you to my oldest girl. Devorah is my most colorful child. She gracefully approaches the mike.

Chapter XII

WHEN SHE WAS FOURTEEN MONTHS old, I was a nervous wreck. You see, her brother who preceded her was a champ at everything. He started swimming at two months and could dive into the deep end by the time he was two. He had over a mouthful of teeth before he was six months. He even talked early. His first word was *ball*.

My second child did not compare. I ran to the doctor, and he tried to make me understand that not only is every child different, but that she was girl. Devorah was happy with the toys around her. Why should she go exploring? She took her first step at eighteen months, and that was very exciting because that meant she could follow her brother around. She was like Old Faithful—every third step, she would plop down on her bottom. She sucked her index finger until she was ten. When we were out and she heard a youngster cry, Devorah started sucking her finger as if to say, *Don't cry; just put your finger in your mouth.* She has a strong singing voice. When the movie *Pocahontas* came out, she wrote down the words and memorized the song, "You think you own every land you land on" and she would hit all the high notes so perfectly. The two older kids were on the swim team, but no matter how much Shimon tried, my little Devorah, his little sister, always beat him by a few seconds.

Her temperament was also different. I remember when I had no husband and was alone with the five children; I received a letter from school that if tuition was not paid by the due date, the children could not continue to attend their classes. Devorah did not make a fuss. Very calmly, she said, "It's okay if I don't go to school. I guess I won't be the president of the junior high." After two weeks, things were worked out, and elections were held. My little Devorah became the president of the whole school.

I had my hands full with her later. Once, when a friend came home from Israel, she got permission to visit. Well, she did not come home, and I had nowhere to begin looking. I had not taken down a name of which friend it was and where she would be. I trusted her that within fifteen to thirty minutes, she would be back. Like a madwoman, I called some of her friends. It was after ten in the evening, and there was no Devorah. I got into the car and went to some of her friends that lived nearby. I can't remember after how many houses, but I walked into Tamara's house, and sure enough, there was my Devorah, innocently watching a movie. If she would have asked permission, why wouldn't I have let her go? I stormed in and asked Devorah to follow me home right now! As I was about to step out of the house, Tamara said in her soft voice, "When I'm a mother, I want to be just like you." That calmed me down just a bit. I only grounded Devorah for a week.

Devorah and I had miscommunication problems many times. David was the president of an organization at one time, and he was master of ceremonies. Needless to say, he was so nervous; he had to give a speech in front of two hundred people. David paid for all the children to be present at the dinner. Devorah forgot and took a babysitting job. I tried to no end to grovel with her to get a replacement, but she came up with a better plan. She asked that we contact her during the party, and if the people came back early enough, I, who was eight months pregnant and all, should come and get her. Well, what in the world was I thinking, and why did I agree? Keep in mind that this was before cell phones. I got up and tried the landline, but there was so much noise that you could not hear your own voice. No luck—no one was picking up the phone.

I could not get Devorah. This happened about three times before I just gave up and tried to enjoy my dinner.

The fund-raiser ended up running late, and when we got home, there was no Devorah! Where could she be? I drove to the apartment where Devorah was babysitting, and to my surprise, she was all prettied up and waiting in the lobby. Devorah was crying. I felt so crushed, and my eyes swelled up; I couldn't say a single comforting word. She is the first Cinderella I know that did not make it to the ball. What happened was that she did not wait for my call; she just assumed that I would come in two hours and pick her up. Until this day, I can't explain to her what happened. Just the thought of her waiting for all those hours, all dressed up so pretty and nowhere to go, makes me want to throw up. The first daughter ever to be stood up by her own mom—what a disgrace! I could not live that down for a very long time.

After high school, Devorah found herself in school in New York. She would rather have been in college in Montreal, but that was her luck. She went to her classes during the day and worked three jobs. She tutored upstairs from her apartment; she worked at the school as an aide; and she worked at Simi Shwarts setting and washing wigs. I remember getting a phone call from the administration, asking if Devorah would be accompanying her class to Israel. I explained that I had no idea there was a trip scheduled. When I got hold of Devorah, I found out that she did not want to ask me for any money. Knowing that I just got remarried to David, and knowing how hard he works, she had raised six hundred dollars all by herself. My husband, even though he is a stepfather for five of my children, treats everyone equally. He loves Devorah very much, and he paid for the rest of the ticket and gave her four hundred dollars spending money.

During the summer, she found herself spending a lot of time with Simi and her family. Simi took a great interest in Devorah. Devorah was in charge of organizing Simi's three-year-old son's party. She was so amazing at decorating cupcakes, and she did a fireman theme, even making her own ladder, painting it, and arranging the cakes on the ladder. She created a masterpiece of a fireman cake.

Simi knew Devorah was a great catch for her brother-in-law. Eli was twenty-five years old, smart, good-looking, and wanted by all the available bachelorettes in the country. But Eli took his time. He went out with fourteen girls before Devorah, and he did not speak to his parents for six months for setting him up with the girl before her. She was so grotesque! Devorah had charm and wit, not to mention an hourglass figure and matching looks, and Eli did marry Devorah. Simi's plan worked—even though on the very first date, when he opened the door for her to get into the car, she slipped and got mud all over her clothes. (We were all peeking from behind the kitchen shades.)

Today, Devorah decorates her house with all the colors on her pallet. That only came about because of Eli. He hated to see her wearing black. Even though she looked stunning in a cute black dress, most of the outfits were just dark colors. He sent her to Mrs. Brach Block in the valley. She works with you and finds out what colors and fabrics you can wear, how to fix your hair, and what color and what kind of jewelry to wear. Devorah introduced me to Brach; the business name is Flying Colors. I have my own album with magnificent arrangements of matching fabrics that I can wear. I found out that I'm a summer, just like Devorah. My shocker was that the colors I mostly stayed away from—copper, ruby, metallic gold and silver, and so forth—were the exact complementary and exotic ones that made me look like a real fashion model. Because of Devorah, I too get my face waxed, and I get pedicures and manicures. I have gotten a facial once in my entire life so far. I don't have the time and extra money to spend when I still have five more children to raise. My husband prefers that I would never have made this discovery of going to a salon and taking care of me and sometimes treating my daughter and daughters-in-law.

I once spent five hundred dollars just on makeup. Devorah, at that time, was the bride, and she had her makeup done. She talked me into having all her sisters and me made up. It was worth it. No wonder they call it makeup. I had false eyelashes and so much paint from the top of my forehead down to my neck. Nowadays I am invited once every three months to Devorah's house for a weekend. She serves us the best bottle of wine and the finest cooked meals. The best part of the deal is that she never lets me bring a thing or allows me to help clean up or serve. I love Eli, her husband. He makes sure my Devorah is loved and taken care of, and it really shows in the atmosphere of their house.

A long time ago, she surprised me with a priceless gift she had schlepped from overseas. Devorah used to live in Israel; her first son was born there. My husband paid for all the children from abroad to come for their sibling's wedding. I met Devorah and her family at LAX. I gave them French croissants from a French bakery. My daughter reciprocated by giving me a box. She said, "Emah, I carried it in my hand luggage, and I made sure nothing would squish it." I opened the box. My face felt hot, my hands weak, and there was silence.

As a child, I spent my first ten years in Israel. My father had to go to the army every six months for training. While he was away, sometimes we ran out of money until the government sent us some.

When I was seven or younger, my mom had searched for hours for some loose change around the house. She looked in desks, coat pockets, and purses. Finally, she was able to scrape together twenty-five cents. She asked me to go to the store and bring her back a can of tomato sauce; she needed to finish dinner. I asked my mom if I could buy myself this Crembo chocolate if there was money left. It is a soft vanilla cookie with a marshmallow cream, covered with chocolate and wrapped with metallic blue-green foil. My mom, without looking at me, answered, "Yes, if there is money left over."

I walked a mile to the store, got the tomato sauce and the Crembo, and put them on the counter. I handed the man the sweaty coins. He smiled and explained that I couldn't buy two things when I only had money for one item. Being a seven-year-old and a chocoholic, I chose the candy. I confidently faced my mom and explained that there was no tomato sauce so I got the candy. My mom did not say a word, just turned to my sister, fourteen months younger, and asked her to go back with me to the store and see if there was no tomato sauce.

The long, agonizing walk with my sister was hell on earth. I pleaded and begged and even told her that she could have the whole candy—just tell Mommy that there was no tomato sauce. My crying and yelling did not move my sister's cold heart. She was on a mission by our mom, and I guess she was so young that she did not understand that sometimes sisters could keep secrets and protect each other. My little sister asked the storekeeper if he had tomato sauce, and he pointed to the rows of nicely stacked red cans on the shelf.

I yelled at the storekeeper, "No, no, tell her you don't have any ... please!" Rachel walked like a soldier, her hands moving from side to side, and I could hardly keep up with her. "Rachel, please don't tell Mommy. I promise I will never lie again. Rachel, come on. Listen to me ..." I was crying hard, wiping my nose and eyes, and trying to keep up with her.

After climbing ninety-eight stairs, my sister entered the one-bedroom apartment and breathlessly reported that there was tomato sauce in the store. The door closed behind me. I walked backward toward the corner. I don't remember when mom got the belt. She must have had it ready before we walked in. She moved slowly toward me, and I could see her lips moving, but I couldn't hear a word she was saying. I was screaming so hard even before the blows of the belt hit me. "Mommy, I'm sorry. Mommy, please ... I'm sorry. I'll never do it again. Mommy, stop! please stop!" I tried not to cry because the more I did, the more blows I would get. Only whimpering sounds escaped uncontrollably. I kept my mouth tightly shut until my mom lost her strength.

When my mom walked away from me, I knew the battle was over. In the corner, I saw this shiny foil. The chocolate marshmallow had been hit harder. You could not recognize what it was before, and you could not salvage it. Since that incident, I did not ever see or eat that candy again, because shortly after that experience, my parents immigrated to Canada.

I had told that story to the kids a long time ago and explained to them that telling the truth and trust are very important rules in life. It's like a wire that is straight—once you bend it, it can't truly be straight again. Once you break the trust or lie, it will be extremely hard to believe you again.

And here in my hands were six Crembos. Devorah proudly said, "Emah, don't share them with anyone. Hide them in the freezer; they are just for you!" I knew that my daughter, in a way, wanted to erase the sad memory and replace it with a beautiful and sweet one. With my wet face, I kissed and thanked her. "Devorah, this is my favorite chocolate. Every time I see or enjoy this treat, I will think of you."

Devorah looks like a princess by the podium. She finishes her speech by quoting a song she and her sisters used to sing to me: "My dear emah, you built a house of Torah ... While you built your own house, you built my home too!" Giving my Devorah a big kiss, I whisper in her ear, "You look prettier than Cinderella on any given day."

Chapter XIII

FROM ALL THE ELEVEN CHILDREN, here comes my child of old. I had her at the age of forty-six. I was considered high risk during the entire pregnancy. The nurses monitored me every two weeks and for one hour every day toward the end.

Today my little Hadassa is all dressed up like a flower girl with a puffy long copper gown. The color and material match the dress Shoshana picked out for me to wear. When could they have planned all this? Shimon walks to the mike and gets Hadassa a chair to stand on. Looking at my little American Jewish doll, I cannot believe I have eleven children. The last one was very hard; I had two miscarriages before that. When Shoshana got married, I had morning sickness that lasted the whole day, and I had to walk her down the aisle. I was two months pregnant with Hadassa. She was born at eleven forty-five on a Monday. G-d gave me a doll to play with in my senior years.

When she was five, Hadassa and I had fun picking a prize after putting in a hard day's work. In the course of two months, Hadassa had to learn addition and subtraction; on top of that, she had to learn to read English and Hebrew. Yes, I had to refresh myself about some old rules I did not know about Hebrew vowels, but in English, there're no rules. My little one (just like me) had to start memorizing how to pronounce some of the words. I feel that my children's successes and failures are mine too.

At this stage of the game, Hadassa and I are in a love/hate relationship. When I reward her, she kisses me and expresses her love to me with trinkets she finds around the house. Then she takes the time to wrap them and uses more Scotch tape than paper. When I have to say something negative—"You must finish your chicken before you can have the brownie" or "Tomorrow is school; no videos" —she says things like, "I hate you" or "I want to go to Devorah's house. I wish she were my mother." Even though I have raised more than a handful of kids, those words are still hurtful. Thank G-d Hadassa is young now—for when she knows she has done something wrong, she apologizes right away, and we kiss and make up. I know I'm going to miss that a lot when she gets older. My other kids as teenagers—forget it. They became total strangers, and sorry was the last thing on their minds. I'm always the first to make up; I feel it's more important to be loved than to be right. The rule is not to let the lows get you too low and not to let the highs get you too high. There has to be a balance. So I try to concentrate on the *good*.

I love rewarding Hadassa because I feel that I too get rewarded. After she had her math facts down pat, we went to the American Girl doll store at The Grove. It's a two-story building. The first floor has a salon for dolls getting their hair done. Yes, the doll hair is real! Upstairs you have the very first doll, Samantha, right down to the newest one, Rebecca; you can even order a doll to look just like you. There is also a section where you and the doll can pick matching outfits. There is a preemie section for infant dolls. There are strollers and so many beautiful accessories, sheets, and quilts … *all for dolls*. They even have a tearoom where you can have a birthday party with your friends, and they bring along their American Girl dolls.

I treated Hadassa to a Rosh Hashanah dress for Samantha, her first doll. Once I paid for the items, the clerk informed me that I must buy a proper hairbrush because a regular one would ruin Samantha's thick brown hair. After looking at the bill, I bargained with Hadassa that this was also going to have to be a big pre-birthday and Chanukah present. Once you are hooked, it doesn't stop.

The next year, I got her a stroller and an outfit that she chose. We saw the bed and dresser for over $118, but I was good and did not reach for my pocketbook. At Pixie Toys on Atlantic, Hadassa and I saw a metal bed with a floral comforter and pillow for the doll. The price was only $35, and I got it for her. Then, at a dollar store, we got an organizer with three drawers, and Hadassa happily played with it. Her favorite time when she is alone is dressing and undressing her dolls, mixing and matching. She has two other friends that also have the same dolls; they come over and play for hours.

So far, Hadassa has ten nephews and three nieces. I got some of my married children to pitch in for an American Girl doll for Channa's fifth birthday. Channa, Shoshana's daughter, is three months younger than Hadassa, and it is always a war! Hadassa feels threatened by her. I remember her once asking me if Channa was going to get married first. I asked her why she thought that. She said, "Well, she is much taller than me." Channa stands a whole head taller than Hadassa, and instead of Hadassa passing down the clothes, we get "hand-me-ups." Hadassa is two, sometimes three, sizes smaller than Channa. Channa talked by the time she was two and a half ... but not our Hadassah. She would point and grunt to get what she wanted.

Another time, when Channa had a pacifier in her mouth, Hadassa, being mischievous as she is, grabbed it and took off giggling around the backyard. A few of us were watching while Channa's father assured her that she should use her words and she would get it back. Channa said, "Please ... please," her arm outstretched. Then she appeared to think about it and said, "Thank you ..." Then she went back to "please ..." Then she said, "Thank you ... please ... thank you ..." Before Channa started to whimper, my husband had to pounce on Hadassa and forcibly pull the pacifier from her clutched hand. Sometimes, on rarer occasions, those two will play together. I hope one day, as they get older, they will be like sisters.

I once had to babysit for Channa and her two younger brothers for fourteen days. I got Channa an American Girl doll stroller for her doll Christy. The girls played pretend for hours. It was fun watching them dress and undress the dolls for different social events that they made up. I love it when they say things like "Pretend I'm sick tomorrow" or "I have to go to New York" or "Pretend my baby can walk now."

While my grandchildren were in school, Hadassa studied multiplication tables up to five. Hadassa was rewarded (with cash, which she saves) for acting maturely and not quarreling with Channa. Hadassa worked very hard, and at the age of seven, she knew her times tables up to six. On her own, Hadassa came up to me and worked on the rest of the times tables because she wanted to pick a matching outfit for her doll and herself.

Because Hadassa is my youngest, I can't leave her alone when I must go places. At three months old, she had a passport to fly to Australia. My Shoshana had given birth to Channa, my first granddaughter. At seven months, she returned with me to Australia when my oldest son got engaged. At six months old she came with me to London. A year later, Hadassa returned with me to celebrate a new grandson's circumcision. What a trip that was. I could have vanished off the face of this earth and no one would have known what happened.

I was catching a taxi from my son's apartment. He made sure to call a reliable one, explaining to me that many foreigners who came to the country couldn't even speak the language, but they all get the job of chauffeuring natives and tourists around. I felt secure with the note with Shoshana's address and phone number and my infant in her car seat next to me. The Russian taxi driver drove for twenty minutes and brought me in front of a huge house at 110 Georgia Street. I looked at the house and explained that this was not my daughter's house. He got agitated quickly and answered, "Yes it is!" I read what was on my paper, and the man said, "Oh, they never said in Newtown." I could feel my stomach in my throat. We drove thirty minutes, and he could not find it. He flagged another cab down. "Do you know how to get to 110 Georgia Street in Newtown?"

The other cab made a sharp U-turn and was right behind our cab.

I transferred my suitcase, baby bag, car seat with baby, and my purse to the backseat of the other car. The cab driver began to question whether I had cash. I explained that I had American money, but if he took me to my daughter, I would gladly bring down some Australian cash for him. I looked carefully at the man driving the car, and sure enough, I felt my goose was cooked! The foreigners my son was trying not to expose me to … Well, I'm Jewish, and the cab driver was Muslim. My son knows how strongly I feel about Israel, and he does not want me discussing my political views with a total stranger. The middle-aged man drove for more than an hour, and he could not find the address. To my surprise, he made a U-turn, pulled up to the curb, and said, "Get out."

I repeated, "Get out? Get … get out where?" I requested that he take me to the police station. He turned me down, and before I could put my infant's car seat on the curb, he drove off. I looked up to the sky, about to thank G-d for saving me from the mouth of a lion, but now what?

There was a man on his balcony of a third-story building, minding his own business and fixing the hinge on his porch door. Out of nowhere, I started yelling, "Excuse me!" I shouted louder, and the man finally looked down at me. I started mumbling and crying at the same time. "I have no idea where I am, and I don't know where to go." The man looked dumbfounded. He agreed to come down and talk to me.

When he did, I explained everything that had happened, telling him that I was totally lost and all I had was this piece of paper with an address. The man took control. He was extremely attractive, a Rock Hudson type! You don't need more of a description than that. I was not thinking; he took the paper out of my hand and said he would be back. Was I crazy? Now I didn't even have a phone number or address of where I was to go. I'd just given the most valuable information away. I had no idea who this man was or what he was doing—or where he had gone. I looked down at my Hadassa, so peacefully sucking her pacifier. My tears automatically stopped; I had to get home! After what seemed like hours but was only twenty minutes, the man came with a black Ford Mustang convertible and proceeded to open the door for me. I felt safe in the backseat with my baby and the new driver. He had a map opened, and away we went. The man's name was David. Oh dear G-d, all my angels are David.

As we drove for over an hour, we got acquainted and found we had a lot in common. We were both overjoyed with our second marriages. He'd finally married his high school sweetheart, the one he'd left behind in England thirty years earlier. They each had two sets of grown children. His wife was a teacher like me, and he was a CPA like my David. David drove around and showed me the university and lovely parks, and then—he couldn't help—he had to drive through the slum areas too. Just like in any ghetto, there were people smoking and drinking, surrounded by graffiti. He informed me that they were from the original aborigines. Today the government is trying hard to educate them, giving them breaks on student loans and even housing. But unfortunately, some don't want to give up their ways and they stay on the reservations. We must have driven at least an hour and a half. The sun was a beautiful orange red. I thought about my kids and how worried they must be. I'd left them at ten in the morning, and now it was past four. David parked the car a couple of times to look at the map. The place where Shoshana lived was a bird reservation, a sanctuary for exotic birds. David pulled up to a dead-end street and turned around. Sure enough, there was Shoshana outside. You could tell she was happy to see me. Her first words out of her mouth were, "I didn't know what to tell Daddy as to what could have happened to you."

I thanked the man and offered one hundred dollars. "Please take it. You must. I will feel so much better for putting you out so much."

He shook his head. "No, this one is on me," he said. "It's not every day you see a damsel in distress." And he drove off.

When Shoshana and I got a chance to talk, she explained to me that this man called her and asked if she had a mother here with a little baby, and then he hung up. She thought I was kidnapped, and that soon he would call back for ransom money. I realized that he must have made a phone call after he took the paper from me. He wanted to know if my story was legit. Shoshana continued, "I had no idea who this person was, and I've been worried for hours. Poor Shimon has no idea where you are."

The last day in Australia, Shimon did not want me in any more taxis; he took me to the mall to buy some souvenirs for the kids back home. As we were walking, my purse got hooked on the stroller. I tried to get it out, and at the same time, a man touched my shoulder. I screamed … then stopped. "No, no, oooooohhhhhhhh. This is him!" The contents of my purse splattered all over the place, and Shimon's body kept bobbing up and down. He didn't seem to know if he should help me pick up my stuff or keep this guy away from me.

The man put his index figure to his mouth and said, "Ssssh. They will think I'm robbing you."

"This is Rock Hudson, the man who saved my life. Actually, this is David. What are the odds of us meeting like this?"

Shimon shook his hands and hugged him. "Thanks to good people like you, my mom is alive today."

When Hadassa was three years old, I treated myself for my fiftieth birthday to a kosher cruise to Alaska. However, I could not bear the thought of leaving Hadassa for even a day, never mind a whole week. My husband agreed, and we took along our daughter Miriam, who was fourteen at the time, to babysit. With Yaacove, Hadassa accompanied us to Hawaii and Maui. My husband and I love it there. We feel it's like the Garden of Eden right here on Earth. I remember the four of us playing twenty questions at the hotel, when we were just passing time before we had to go to the airport. Each of us got a turn, and now it was Hadassa's turn. We asked the following questions:

"Is it alive?"

She said no.

"Is it a person?"

She said yes.

"Is it is a man?"

"Did we see it on our vacation?"

She said yes.

"Is he famous?"

She said yes.

The questions went on and on, but we could not guess. Finally, twelve-year-old Yaacove shouted, "We give up!"

Triumphantly, she said, "It's Pearl Harbor. We saw his grave yesterday … remember?"

We all laughed so hard that our sides ached. My husband gets such pleasure repeating that story to family and friends. He might save it for her bat mitzvah speech.

Hadassa's favorite pastime is reading. In school, as with the other children, she has Reading Counts. She gets points for every book she reads, and she takes a comprehension test afterward. Her teacher expressed how proud she is that Hadassa has forty-six points this year. Hadassa responded, "I can't wait to be like Yaacove; he has over a thousand points." I still enjoy reading to her before she goes to bed, but she is often interested in the books I read. She makes me tell her parts of the story as I'm reading, and then we sympathize with the different characters.

Hadassa is sensitive to what people say, and she has the right answer to make you feel great. The other day, when she and I were watching Pennina's wedding video on the computer, I worriedly commented, "At your wedding, Hadassa, I will be too old to dance."

Hadassa quickly answered, "Emah, look at all those older people dancing around … You will not be old. You will have more energy than any of them!" Hadassa is truly a blossoming flower. She is also learning to love G-d.

The hardest thing to teach each of the children is to feel the love of G-d in everything around us. But each one, on his or her own, just like Hadassa, grows each day and relates to the Creator differently. Some of my kids run to help another without once thinking how much it will require of them. Some run to prayer on time; others help in the kitchen and cook for two hundred members to save on catering costs. Hadassa, at this age, sits next to me every Shabbat morning and says six different prayers. She notices the words and finds a similarity between the words she studies in school and her Torah. She loves all the Bible stories and wishes to be a teacher just so she can tell stories to her students.

Now Hadassa stands so proud and begins to sing a song that all her sisters used to sing around the house growing up: "My Dear Emah!" The whole crowd is singing. I can't believe what I'm seeing and hearing. What a surprise. After they finish, I am asked to get up and face the crowd. My life partner is standing next to me.

CHAPTER XIV

Now LET'S HEAR FROM MY Romeo, the one and only, my David. I'm next to him by the mike, but I can't hear what he is saying. This man is the real reason for my happiness; he keeps me smiling. Before I was introduced to David, I had to be strong for my children. I had to pretend I was happy, but I was all alone. My children were little. They did not understand the ugliness of divorce. Cruel as it was, it was necessary. It took a whole lot of adjusting, and the worst part was giving the kids up to go over to the side of the enemy (their father, the nameless). The boys went one weekend, the girls another, and then they all went one weekend a month. I was dead without them! When they went to the other side, they took my heart and my reason for living. It was hard to bear that one weekend a month.

Once I tried to get drunk. I poured myself a large glass of red wine and wondered what it would be like if I got nice and numb. I would forget my troubles and sleep the whole Sunday away until the kids came back. It did not work! Just as I was about to get comfortable and take my first sip, that darn phone rang. It was an old friend looking for "the nameless." The young man was a mutual married friend, and when he got wind that I was divorced, he let his real feelings about the children's father flow. We talked about his character and his values. Best of all, we laughed and shared the same adjectives, and we ended up discovering that we both disliked him! It turned out that he too had some smoldering smoke to put out. After we talked for two hours, I felt great. I could not believe myself. I poured a perfectly good glass of wine down the bathroom sink.

Another Sunday that I was alone, I took a ride to the Santa Monica Pier. I walked to the secluded part of the beach and let the ocean water touch my toes. Looking at the strength of the ocean, I wanted to breathe it all in. In my hands, I was holding a gold twenty-pound leather album. I opened each page and then dropped the album on the sand. I saw my sister and father, who are no longer in this world, and I cried aloud, "Please come and take me. I have nothing left. I don't want to live like this!" I felt cold ocean water come and cover my knees; I scooted back a yard or two. On the first page, I saw my radiant smile and how I looked. I remembered my mom copying the picture of this four-layer lace wedding dress from a magazine that I had brought her. She perfected it. It looked better than in the picture. It took my mother a month or so to design and sew it, and I used to put on different parts of the dress—just the top or just a sleeve, then just the bottom. Each time, I would twirl like a ballerina. I was a queen just for one day.

I buried my head in the three thousand dollars' worth of pictures and just let it all come out. The ocean had a different plan; it wanted me to stop feeling sorry for myself, so it sprayed me with such a huge wave that you could not tell I was crying. I got up. I pulled apart the eight-by-ten pictures of my album and tossed them one by one, like Frisbees, into the ocean. Each throw was with such gusto that my arms hurt. I had seventy-five pages. Each picture bobbed on top of the water and then was dragged to my feet as if giving me a last kiss, saying good-bye and then disappearing far away, never to be seen again. I was exhausted but happy. It was like throwing my cancer, my sickness, into the ocean, making me feel stronger.

I began thinking of my father, the beautiful things he had brainwashed me with: "Yael, be like a wrapped present! You want your husband to be the first to touch you, kiss you, and look at you. If everything is open, then what is so exciting? Everything is exposed and used up. Be a rose that is on its vine. Only let your true love pluck you; no one wants a wilted flower." After listening to the same exact words over and over, like a broken record, they started to be part of me. I decided to be a good girl, and I was. I did nothing wrong. I did not stay out all night; I did not drink or smoke anything. I was good, and it upsets me that I obviously saved myself for the wrong guy. I'd wasted nine and a half years of my life.

One time I was crying so hard, unfortunately in front of family aunts and uncles—it was my aunt Sarah's fiftieth wedding anniversary party—and there was Josef, my first cousin, who was studying to be a psychologist. My cousin bravely asked, "Yael, why are you crying? Do you think it's a mistake?" (He was referring to the divorce.)

"No way!" I yelled back. "No way! Uh-uh!" I let out a loud noise of frustration and wiped my wet face. "It's just that I'm not a virgin anymore. I'm all used up."

Josef saw me falling apart, and before I could start my next good cry, he politely said, "We can fix that."

I stopped crying and began laughing so hard, and I could tell, as he continued, that he was feeling proud of himself for getting me out of the dumps and in a better mood.

"Yes," he said, "you can have an operation and be a virgin again."

I retaliated by saying, "Nu-uh!"

"Yeah, it can get sewn up just like a turkey!"

That was it. I could not cry after that. It was like switching gears. I was happy and giggling. I knew I could always count on Josef to make me feel good.

The next time I was alone, it was not as bad. Of course I missed those kids tons, but I decided I must live for them. I used to invite a girlfriend to sleep over, or I would go to a friend's house for the weekend. I started to attend Torah classes. I took up sewing again, which I had not done in ten years. At that time, I was a teacher for elementary students, and during those dark times, I got this new passion and energy for life. I put on plays; I sang with my classes; I took them on special trips. I started reading books about friendship, marriage, love, happiness, and most important, I started loving me. I did it! I was going to fight and win. Sometimes after putting the children to bed, I could not sleep, so I would get out the book of Psalms and read certain chapters. I wished more than anything that I would find a man that would love me and, most of all, love my children. After two years of praying, G-d remembered me and sent me an angel.

Blending a family is not easy in any way. In fact, the odds are against second marriages working out, especially with kids. The common denominator between David and me was praying, praying, and a lot of praying. When I was told to go out with this man, I asked how old he was. The matchmaker kept avoiding the question. I persisted. I then protested, "No way. I will not go out with a man twelve years my age."

At first, David's matchmaker would not disclose how many children I had from the previous marriage. When he found out, he yelped, "No way will I go out with someone with five children, someone who looks like a fat washwoman." I was in no way fat, try ninety-five pounds, and I had an hourglass figure.

Well, after talking to me for two and a half hours in the ninety-degree weather, he finally went to get us some apple juice, but when he proceeded to hand mine to me, his hands shook. Immediately, I knew he liked me. I can go on and on or write a book on how I survived. But one thing is for sure: he is an angel—when he is asleep! Just joking. But when he is up, I'm the angel. That way we do not argue. A boss of mine once told me that it's better to be loved than to be right.

When things get me down and I'm overwhelmed, David cracks a joke, and I laugh loudly for a long time. Speaking about laughing, before I married David, when I would smile, I covered my mouth because I was embarrassed by my teeth. Here I was, thirty-three, and for the past twenty-three years, I would only eat on the right side of the mouth. You see, my parents did not believe in dentists. But they believed in them enough to allow them to pull teeth so when I got a cavity, the dentist just pulled my tooth out. The left side of my mouth was missing three teeth. David got me to a dentist who happened to be his best friend, and within two years, I had a million-dollar smile. Now when I open my mouth, I feel alive, no shame, and I show off my new happy laugh.

Thank G-d for our eleven beautiful children, but to this day, I can't find the secret ingredient for making all the children content and in a good place at the same time. My oldest son is thirty-seven now, and as soon as I see him, I have to put on my invisible boxing gloves or have my checkbook handy. One of my daughters bought a house; another is struggling and can't put food on the table. One gets a 96 percent on his history final; one does not want to put on a hat and jacket during religious services. One gets an A minus on an oral religion test; one reads books until all hours of the night and then does not turn in complete assignments. One just passed a math test; another thinks there is nothing wrong with talking on Facebook when it's past midnight. My little one wants my jewelry so she can give it to her best teacher; one has fluid behind his inner ear and will need tubes for the fourth time.

Everyone needs me, all at the same time. Someone is always mad at me! I wish the kids and my beloved could coordinate some day when they were all mad and give me some weekdays that they would know to be extra, extra nice to me, when no one was allowed to complain or to be mean.

One time when I was in the kitchen cooking, I happened to talk about one of my husband's friends (I was making small talk; actually, I had a brainstorm, a great match for this client), not noticing that my spouse was worried about this guy's taxes. With a flash, he snapped, acting, let us say, inhuman, as if a strange wind had come over him. I wondered if a plea of temporary insanity would stand up in court. I was so hurt, and as my eyes welled up, I went toward the sink and ran the water as if I were washing some dishes.

A short time passed, and David walked close behind me and whispered, "I'm waiting." I turned around and he said, "I'm sorry. I'm really sorry. It's just that this person is important. I can't mess up, and my computer has a virus *again*!"

He went away, and five minutes later, he came back. I was covered with flour, making bread for Friday night dinner. I was caught off guard by his remark: "You are costing us money." Now I wanted to retaliate. Over the past twenty years, I had learned to be quiet. But boy, when I got ignited, it was like a firecracker taking off, with no stop in sight. Unfortunately, I did not have too many good role models. Again, my parents were from India. Not to say that they were hot-tempered people; on the contrary, they were highly emotional, caring, and vocal in a good way. At any time, they would take their shirts off their backs for you. For every one of my pregnancies, right up until the last, I wished for an Indian midwife. Yes, G-d did listen. Not only are they soft-spoken, but their hands are very healing, especially when you are having big contractions. My first cousin's parents are also Jews from India. Her father married my mother's oldest sister (my aunt). I never saw UncleBenny (that's what I used to call him) lose his composure; he was like my dad—extroverted, optimistic, and so loving and warm. But in my house, things were different.

While I was growing up, my father always had to give in, whether my mom was right or wrong. She'd scream loudly and carry on for hours; she'd throw everything in her closet into an open suitcase and then continue screaming as if someone were attacking her. This went on until my dad somehow said the magic words. Every time it was different, but then they would make up, and no matter what time of day or night it was, I had to clean everything up and get it back in order. When I was in my late teens, Daddy and I had many talks about my mom's outbursts and mood swings, but he did not believe in psychology or therapy. Something was definitely wrong with Mom! Daddy did not believe in divorce either. He could not do that to us—his whole life was us. Growing up like this, life was hard for me—the exposure to violence and name-calling, all done in their native tongue so I would not understand. Oh, that's what they thought! Unfortunately, I can't speak Marti or Hindu, but I do know two handfuls of swear words.

I used to be in bed and sometimes fall asleep to their continued bickering. In the morning, I'd get up like a mouse so as not to upset anyone and get my sister, who was only fourteen months younger than my brother, who was seven years younger than I was, ready for school. I would get them on the bus as quickly as possible and pray the whole day that when I came back, Mommy and Daddy would be happy and still together.

As an adult with my own kids, I do blame my dad too. Even though he did not start the fights or add to the fire, I feel he should have protected us better. From the first fight he had with mom, he should have put his foot down, telling her never to yell in front of the children and never to raise her voice. When I got married to David, I had to learn from scratch how to make a marriage work. And that is exactly what it is: *work*! A good marriage does not just happen. Two people have to be interested and committed. I learned how to be good. I had to hold my animal instinct back.

Now … what was David talking about? Was he complaining about the Kleenex I was using or the water I was pretending to use? I just yelled, "What?"

With a big smile on his face, he said, "I can't work if I'm sad. You're my only friend; please be nice to me."

I laughed so hard. "You're sad? You're sad?" I love it when he is wrong!

I once asked him to cover my Costco check and other nooks and crannies (stuff) I bought for the kids. He complained, throwing his hands up in the air and shouting, "I gave you the money to cover that."

I gently rationalized, "You gave me six hundred dollars twice: once to cover airline tickets for New York for five hundred and eighty-three dollars; the other time for six hundred dollars for credit cards."

He looked at me with disgust, and I knew I'd better walk away. I did, but first I slammed some bedroom doors shut, then put on loud music, and finally, well, the poor laundry basket … I kicked it so hard that if I were on a soccer field, I know I would have made a goal. I watched as it made a loud noise and made my husband jump. I'd just made my point. I'd scored! I grabbed my pocketbook and went for a walk, slamming the front door shut behind me. At the bank, the teller printed receipts for the two times I had made six-hundred-dollar deposits.

David called me on my cell. "How come you didn't say good-bye?"

I whispered where I was and said that I had proof of only two deposits, on October 25 and 26. He was regretful and said my favorite three words: *I love you.*

Raising these ankle biters (as my husband called them when they were young) is a real job! Not nine to five—it's twenty-four/seven! Thanks to David's profession and flaming love for the crumb crunchers (another name he used to call the young ones), he allowed me to be *emah*—and stay at home with my kids. Being with them, I got to enjoy life and point out to them when the wind blows and let them watch the leaves fall. Not one leaf falls from a tree unless G-d ordains it from above. The leaf disconnects from the branch and gracefully, like a ballerina, floats all the way to the earth. I have time to think of G-d, because even if I have had a bad day, I can go outside and feel the fresh air, hear the birds, feel touched by the warm sun, and see the colors all around me, making my entire body relax. I know G-d loves me. I'm happy and joyful doing my duty as an emah. There is no better reward than to give birth and raise a good child like a strong tree—a tree that can bend a little when attacked by a storm or stand straight and upright when necessary. I know the trick is not to let the ups get you too up, and not to let the downs get you too down, especially with all that's on my plate. *Balance!*

I remember Devorah asking why so many children. "Why did you not stop after Shimon and me? You would have had one boy and one girl." I asked her to picture a Maserati or Corvette. They are beautiful cars to race or just use for a leisurely drive. But what happens if you own an expensive automobile just for show? You get no use out of it. So too I feel that within the sanctity of marriage, a woman's body is for reproducing.

There was a time when I did not want additional kids. After the third child, I quit. I had three children who were three and under, all fourteen months apart. The baby bag I carried was bigger than I was. Everything was times three: three pacifiers, three bottles, three diapers, and so on. Then Shoshana turned three, and I decided to have more. I had Larry and then Pennina. I got remarried to David. His daughter Sophie was six months older than Pennina. Then I did it again! Four years of marriage and I had three new kids, two of them eleven months apart. Stop! Stop! Stop! *No more kids.*

I remember planning a trip to my homeland of Israel. I had not been back in thirty years. We both went, just the two of us, for seventeen and a half days. Daily, David went early to pray by the Wailing Wall, and he came back with fresh-baked bread. We rented a room from a ninety-one-year-old woman. She fixed us breakfast every morning and ice cream for a midnight snack if we wanted. After two days of napping when we wanted to, going out on the town, and just having the time of our lives, we missed the children terribly. Before Shabbat, we called home. Shoshana answered; she was sixteen at the time. She was overwhelmed; she demanded that we come home right away and said that nothing was the same without us. Everything fell on her shoulders. My mom was there with our oldest son, who had the keys to drive the kids, but Devorah, well, I guess she was not much help. We missed the kids so we called after Shabbat. The children were happy overall, and most importantly, Shoshana reassured us that if we wanted to, we could stay longer. Both of us felt that if someone were to pay us a million dollars, we would not change our minds about our children being in our lives.

Before the trip, I had this dream. My husband and I were hiding in a huge haystack in some barn during the Holocaust. Suddenly, the door opened, and in shone this bright flashlight. We peeked, and there was a man in uniform with two children. I could not see faces, but one child was in beige from head to toe, the other beige from head down to the knees. The man began to speak. "If you want to save their lives, come at six thirty in the evening. If you don't come, they will be killed!" I didn't know what to make of the dream.

Now that I was in Israel, I convinced David to visit the Bali Rebbe in Benai Brak. It was difficult to get an appointment with the rebbe, but finally we got to see him at nine at night. His gracious wife, Sarah, welcomed us. Then the big moment came—we were sitting just a few inches in front of him. I had met with the Bali Rebbe in 1988, just after my father died and when I chose to be alone with five children.

The rebbe did a very strange thing. He studied the piece of paper with each of my precious children's names and then asked how old Devorah was. My second child, Devorah, was eight at the time. Then, just like that, I was escorted out. I could not understand what kind of a blessing that was. For days and months, I walked around looking at billboards with the number eight. All of a sudden, a license plate would have two eights or the bill would come out to eight dollars even at the store.

A short time later, in 1990, I met and married David. He had one child, and I had five—together we were eight. I later mothered three more children. That brought the grand total of children that I had given birth to to eight. Then I went to visit the rebbe again, in 1996, eight years after my first visit. A coincidence? I don't think so.

This time, the rebbe scanned over the names of our blended family, and he asked, "How old is Sophie?"

I told him she was ten.

David was venturesome enough to ask if we should move the whole family to Israel.

The Bali Rebbe answered, "Not now. When you win the lottery."

I went out on a limb and asked for an explanation of my dream. He became serious and started to gesture with his hands, and not once looking at me, he started to speak.

"This dream comes from above. You were supposed to have these children in another life. It did not materialize. So G-d sent you both back down to complete your job, but the second time it has to be a bit difficult."

So, to make a long story short, I gave birth to a beautiful son that year, and five years later, I had a daughter. I gave birth to ten kids, but together we have eleven. Thank G-d!

David gives me nice presents for all the hard work I do. Again, for my fiftieth birthday, we went on a kosher cruise to Alaska and enjoyed a week of our beds made up for us and a chocolate bar at night. We ate around ten meals a day: breakfast, snack, lunch, teatime snack, supper, snack, midnight snack … It was so much like living the life of a queen. We ate duck, ribs, crepes of all sorts, chicken, and breads of different colors. And then there were the trips to Cabo San Lucas and Hawaii, but I did have to cook every meal, so Alaska was a welcoming break out of the same rut.

The music starts, and my David has stopped talking. The audience applauds. David begins to sing his favorite from Sonny and Cher: "I Got You Babe!" The guests join in, and for a grand finale, he says, "Happy sixtieth birthday, Yael."

On the ride home in a white limo, David notices the bright, perfect-shaped moon. While we both stare up at the sky, simultaneously we mutter, "We both got a second chance." David discloses to me that he has another surprise. Wondering what it can be, I then stop thinking and let my eyes close a little. Nothing can top this evening. The limo stops. We walk in giggling like newlyweds. I am instructed to stay in the kitchen. Five minutes or so pass, and I think that I have to get dinner out for the next day.

David walks in and puts on a tape. The music starts. David can't dance for more than three seconds or he gets dizzy. But we get into position and laugh, singing along to Dean Martin: "When the moon hits your eye like a big pizza pie, that's amore." It's been more than three seconds, and now I'm turning and still holding David's hands, and he brings me around and across … What? He actually dips me.

"Hey, when this did happen? How come?"

He laughs and discloses to me what he learned with Larry, and then he continues, "Do you like it?"

I answer affirmatively. I love to dance! As I swing around again, I notice people peeking into our kitchen windows. Oh my, there they are, all eleven with their families. The partying continues through that evening, and it does not end. I will forever remember it in my heart.

Me, well … I am proud to be called *Emah*.

Thank G-d!